In a world that focuses more on throwing a wedding than building a marriage, Rebecca VanDoodewaard provides excellent wisdom and insight to help women carefully consider the type of spouse they hope to marry. With kindness and truth woven together, she unpacks the long-term mental, emotional, physical and spiritual impact of marriage. This book is a valuable and much-needed resource for women.

Melissa Kruger
Author, *The Envy of Eve*
Charlotte, North Carolina

If you are a single woman, this may be the most important book you read this year. Rebecca VanDoodewaard writes with clarity, brevity, conviction and passion on an area of the Christian life that many overlook until it is too late. Heed the warnings in this book, be fortified by its encouragements, and give an ear to its sound biblical advice. As a pastor in a university church, I would place this book in the hands of every single young woman I could. And as a father, this is a book that I will ask my daughter to prayerfully read from cover to cover.

Jason Helopoulos
Assistant Pastor
University Reformed Church
East Lansing, Michigan

Finally, a book for the woman wondering if she has found the right man for a life-long commitment. In *Your Future 'Other Half': It matters whom you marry* a woman will find ways to look into a man's heart before she entrusts hers completely to him at the altar. Rebecca VanDoodewaard offers wise counsel to help women make a biblically informed decision, because whom you marry really does matter! Every chapter offers solid biblical ways to pursue intimacy with insightful questions about a man's spiritual, intellectual, emotional, physical, and relational capacities. I think the study questions at the end should be required of all couples coming for pre-marriage counsel! They will help couples think through both the internal and external dimensions of their life together. This book is a must-read for any woman thinking about marriage, in a marriage now, or helping others towards a life-long biblical romance that echoes the love of Christ for His Bride and her joyous 'Yes!' to Him. Buy it! Read it! Use it! I know I will.

Jani Ortlund
Author of *Fearlessly Feminine*
Executive Vice President
Renewal Ministries
Franklin, Tennessee

YOUR
FUTURE
'OTHER HALF'

It matters whom you marry

REBECCA VANDOODEWAARD

CHRISTIAN
FOCUS

Scripture quotations are from The Holy Bible, English Standard Version, copyright © 2001 by Crossway Bibles, a division of Good News Publishers. Used by permission. All rights reserved. ESV Text Edition: 2007.

Rebecca VanDoodewaard is a freelance editor. Her husband William VanDoodewaard is ordained in the Associate Reformed Presbyterian Church and serves as associate professor of church history at Puritan Reformed Theological Seminary in Grand Rapids, Michigan. They blog together at thechristianpundit.org.

paperback ISBN 978-1-78191-298-0
epub ISBN 978-1-78191-330-7
Mobi ISBN 978-1-78191-331-4

Published in 2014
reprinted in 2014
by
Christian Focus Publications, Ltd.
Geanies House, Fearn, Ross-shire,
IV20 1TW, Scotland, United Kingdom.
www.christianfocus.com

Cover design by Daniel van Straaten

Printed by Nørhaven, Denmark

CONTENTS

For my mother-in-law,
who raised my favorite man in the world;

And for my parents, who talked me into that first 'date.'

Introduction

A guy once told me that Jane Austen novels were just well-written harlequins without the bedroom scenes. He meant that the basic plots follow the same pattern that all romance novels seem to: girl wants true love, looks for it, has one or two emotional mishaps, finds true love. But Austen's novels actually contain many more dysfunctional relationships than healthy ones: for every Lizzie and Mr. Darcy, there is a Charlotte and Mr. Collins or a Mr. and Mrs. Bennett. For every Jane and Mr. Bingley there is a Wickham and Lydia or a Mr. and Mrs. Hurst. Sadly, the novels are true to real life. Our world is full of unhappy marriages; more people live unhappily ever after than otherwise.

This is even true in some Christian communities. Unfortunately, single believers are often less diligent and perceptive than Lizzie Bennett in evaluating potential spouses. While this book does not want to give you a checklist for your relationship, it does aim to encourage you to think about marriage in such a way that you will be able to make a wise and biblically informed decision about the person that you marry. Apart from salvation, no other decision will have such an impact on your life.

But why does it matter so much? Won't everything be all right as long as you are in love? Isn't every single Christian male a potential spouse? Actually, no! And that is because God created marriage to be a relationship (the *only* relationship) in which two become one. This is true physically, but it is also true spiritually, emotionally, relationally, and mentally. A husband and wife become one—intertwined to the extent that after years or decades of marriage it is difficult to do or say anything to the one that the other does not immediately feel. This is why it is so important that you pursue this kind of intimacy only with the right person—because you and he will be joined in profound ways that are difficult to understand even after years of experience. Our culture uses the term 'intimacy' almost exclusively in reference to sexual activity. Of course, intimacy can include sexual closeness, but its meaning is much deeper than that. Intimacy in a marriage is intensely personal closeness that includes spiritual, emotional, intellectual, and physical togetherness.

If you are unmarried, it is difficult to grasp the implications that this intimacy brings. This book will help you start thinking through exactly that. Using examples from church history and my own experience as a pastor's daughter and professor's wife, measured against biblical principles, we will look at the areas of personhood that marriage and a spouse will change, and the implications that those changes can have, for better or for worse.

If you are already in an unhappy marriage, there are ways to get help. Depending on the nature and depth of the problem, you may need the support of your extended family, the counsel of your pastor, or even the protection of police.[1] But if you are not married, please don't put yourself in such a situation just because you have not thought things through first. True, you cannot predict or foresee every possible situation in a relationship or the changes that a spouse will go through after the wedding. That is why wedding vows bind a man and wife together 'from this day forward, for better, for worse, for richer, for poorer, in sickness and in health, to love

---

1 See the appendix at the back of this book for resources for someone in a difficult marriage.

and to cherish, till death us do part, according to God's holy law.' A change in your spouse or any other future circumstance is something that you cannot avoid by careful thought and planning before engagement, and no circumstance, apart from biblical grounds, can terminate a marriage.[2] But, being in a bad marriage and getting into an avoidable bad marriage are two different things.

You may be wondering, can't God redeem a bad marriage? Can't God use you to change your spouse for the better? Most definitely—how gracious! He has done these sorts of things in the past and He is doing them now. He also used the prostitute Rahab to help His people conquer Jericho, converted John Newton when he was a slave trader, and allows people to survive airplane crashes. But that does not mean that it is moral to engage in prostitution with the goal of helping the church, to buy and sell slaves with the hope of personal revival, or to crash your plane so that you can see God's power. No right-thinking person would do those things. Yet, many Christians get married to people whom they have no business marrying.

Why does this happen? Many times, people pick a spouse without thinking through the implications

---

2   These are adultery and desertion. See Jay Adams' *Marriage, Divorce, and Remarriage in the Bible: A Fresh Look at What Scripture Teaches* (Grand Rapids: Zondervan, 1980) for a full discussion of biblical thought on divorce.

of life-long intimacy with this person. Some women marry because they feel sorry for a guy; others because they see no better option. It's common for young people to marry simply because of sexual pressure or passion, not truly considering the greater implications for the rest of their lives. Many girls marry because they are afraid of some aspect of singleness. They haven't grasped that it's far better to be single for life than to marry someone who will make your life a burden. Singleness can be great; a bad marriage is crushing. And while a stable marriage requires that you be willing to do your utmost to make it work, a thriving marriage requires that both husband and wife work together and for each other in order to be a picture of Christ and the Church. Although a difficult marriage *can* create spiritual fruit in one spouse, it is not something to choose. And single people often cannot see trouble coming until it's too late.

This came home to me one day as my husband and I ate dinner with a youth group. Three teens sat across from us at the table—two guys and a girl. One guy was a computer geek with glasses. The other was a college student with slightly cooler hair and clothes. The girl was obviously with him. But while the computer geek was busy serving everyone at the meal, clearing plates and garbage, the college student got angry with the girl for a small accident

13

and poured red juice over her leather jacket and white shirt in revenge. She had picked the wrong guy, and the juice didn't seem to change her mind. She is in for some grief if that relationship continues, especially if it leads to marriage; intimacy with a selfish, angry man will destroy much more than her clothing. She is thinking in the short term without accounting for the long term.

If you are single, you can't hear this too often: *whom you marry matters*. You might think that the way he treats you now isn't so bad. But it's not going to get better after the wedding. You might think that he'll change. It's possible, but most people don't. You might think that you'll be able to minister to him and help him. It's possible, but if you can't change him now, then there's no reason to expect that you will be able to in the future, and after marriage, you will be vulnerable yourself. A husband should lead and cherish you, not need your counsel for basic personality or behavior issues. It is good and right to want to minister to another person, and no future spouse will be perfect in every area. But there are ways to minister to people that don't involve dating them! What matters is not that your boyfriend is perfect, but that in major life areas he is standing on a firmly biblical footing.

What will help you decide whom to marry? Is he growing in Christ-likeness and helping you do the same? He does not have to score 100 per cent in every area, but he does have to be headed in the right direction on important issues. A healthy trajectory is vital. That is what you need to look for in each area. Is he heading in a bad direction or a biblical one? Is he doing so intentionally or by default? Ben Franklin said, 'Keep your eyes wide open before marriage, half shut afterwards.' This is the 'wide open' part.

Life does not end at marriage. Instead, marriage shapes life after the wedding. Getting married is not, by itself, a worthy life-goal. Your goal right now should not be to get married, but to make sure, first, that your own life is on the kind of biblical trajectory that shows growth in grace. That is also the best preparation for marriage. You should also consider how your development as a Christian will be buttressed and facilitated and sped up by marriage—by your relationship with a particular person with whom you may some day become one.

Before we begin, I want to be clear: this book cannot give you the ultimate Potential Husband Check List, Dating Strategies that Work, or a Perfect Marriage Pattern that you can hold up to your boyfriend to see if he fits. No book can do that for you, because every man is different, every woman is different, and so every relationship will look different. Martin and Katie Luther were a radically different couple from Martyn and Bethan Lloyd-Jones. Both were solid, loving marriages with husbands leading, wives submitting, and both spouses serving Christ. Neither couple worried about 'compatibility'. They loved Christ and each other: their compatibility came in living that out. But being in the Luther home would have been a very different experience from being in the Lloyd-Jones home, simply because personality, education, circumstance, and a host of other factors shape each marriage into something unique. This book, then, offers no formula.

What this book can do is help you grasp the effects of a marriage and ask some questions about what that might look like for you. Unless a married person is very frank with you, you can't understand how much a husband will influence your entire life. Every area of your life will be impacted deeply. Intimacy in a bad marriage is a dark thing. It is a source of grief and pain and stifling of personhood. But the opposite of bad intimacy is not living parallel lives as individual adults. Lack of intimacy is sterile. It does not produce; it simply permits. The opposite of intimacy in a bad marriage is not lack of intimacy, but intimacy in a good marriage. This kind of intimacy is a wonderful thing. It is a source of joy and comfort and energy and creativity. Cultivating intimacy with a husband is part of God's design for marriage, and so it brings blessing. But you must not marry someone with whom you cannot actively pursue intimacy in a biblical context.

Whom you marry matters not only because it will affect your health, make you sad or happy, create fear or security, but also because it will hinder or enable you to live a life of Christian service. Christian marriage, by God's design, should multiply abilities, fruitfulness, and service, not absorb all of your time, energy, and thought. It should be a source of joy, a spurring one another on to love and good works (Heb. 10:24). Of course, it is true that intimacy with even the best earthly husband will have *some* negative impact on you, simply because every Christian husband is still a sinner until he is glorified in Heaven. No marriage is all good or all bad. The question is whether the overall patterns of a spouse's belief and behavior are conducive to the health of a marriage. Pastor and theologian Derek Thomas warns us, 'He may be, let's say, 6'2 and 175 pounds, have green eyes, a great body and make a bundle of money. He may even drive a Porsche! Yes, and hell may come along with a relationship! ...It's all very well to fall in love with a hunk, but you have to ask, "A hunk of what?"'

Asking good questions about a potential spouse can help you sort this out. Will your husband's interactions with your body, mind, and soul tend towards health, sanctifying you? Since the will of God is your sanctification (1 Thess. 4:3), you must marry someone who makes you want to be more like Jesus and who can help you become more like Jesus. Your marriage matters not only to you, not only to your family, not only to the church, but also to the world. A married couple's relationship will either be a living picture of Christ and the church, or it will be a living lie about Christ and the church. Even Paul described this as a profound mystery (Eph. 5:32). Will your marriage be one that shines gospel love into the world, or one that adds to the darkness? This book will help you think about that.

In the chapters that follow, we will look at some of the ways that marriage will affect five areas of living: spiritual, emotional, physical, mental, and relational. We will also look at ourselves to think about our readiness to be helpmeets: are we up for the challenge? There is a chapter on love, to help us identify some unbiblical and unhealthy patterns of thinking. A chapter on resources includes a list of helpful books about marriage and study questions that can help you evaluate your own relationship in real time.

God might not have marriage in store for you. But if He does, it's my prayer that this book will enable you to carefully weigh the potential effects of a potential spouse: to weed out the Wickhams and Collinses, because happiness in marriage is not merely a matter of chance. It will affect your time on earth and eternity, so it is a matter that deserves our grave consideration.

1

How to use this book

It is obvious, right? Read the book, mentally measure up the guys you know. But that's where we girls often go wrong—in our heads. It's really easy to create evaluations, conversations, and relationships in our minds that don't always correspond to reality. Perhaps we discuss the options with girlfriends, a sister, or a mom, but the person with the most to say to us is, well, us, as we listen to the thoughts in our heads all day.

That's where other people come in. Please do not use this book in isolation. God gives us two main groups of human resources to help us navigate the Christian life: family and church. Older people, wiser people, godlier people who know you and the fellow you have in mind are invaluable in this situation. Are you familiar with the song in *The Sound of Music* where Liesl admits that she needs someone older and wiser to help her through the strange world of interested men? She was right. What she was blind to is that a seventeen-going-on-eighteen-year-old was not what she needed. She needed her dad! Liesl's father saw through Rolfe in a minute, while it took a Nazi uniform for her to clue into what he was really like. '"Love", or "being in love,"' Derek Thomas points out, 'makes us lose touch with reality.'

So please, as you read through this book, start talking to the mature Christians in your life: ask them to shepherd you through this process. Consider your approach to marriage in the context of Christian fellowship. If you have mature Christian parents, recognize them as God's gift to you as you prepare for marriage. Allow your father to do the work of a father as he does some scouting to check out the guy who wants to marry his little girl. My dad did not hesitate to call up the pastors, bosses, and mentors of his daughters' boyfriends to find out what they were really like. We appreciated it: he did it to protect us, not annoy us. I had a friend whose mother required her boyfriend to submit police background checks and credit reports to her; she didn't know the fellow and wanted to make sure that he wasn't a con-artist, criminal, or in debt. That's a good thing! It also speaks to the seriousness of joining oneself to a spouse. Though these kinds of precautions might make you uncomfortable in the moment, they could save you decades of grief.

If your parents are not mature Christians, go hunting for some in your local church.[1] When you are under the spiritual authority of a faithful pastor and elders, you are protected and helped in many ways. If you do not have a father who is willing to screen guys graciously, a good pastor should be. If you need guidance in this area and do not have parents or other close relatives to provide it, your church family should be an ally. Ask older Christians to help you discern whether or not a particular fellow is marriage material. If you aren't dating anyone right now, start having conversations about these issues with older adults in your congregation, and find out what has—and has not—worked for them in these areas.

Even when you do have parents who can help you walk through this stage of life in a biblical way, the local church is vital. Families have blind spots and need support. That is why input from Christian adults who know you but are not related to you

---

1   If you are a Christian but not a member of a local, gospel-proclaiming evangelical church, the appendix has suggestions on how to find one.

is so helpful. A married couple with a growing relationship with each other and the Lord is ideal. They are usually happy to help younger members of the congregation who are thinking through life-changing decisions. One pastor's wife I know was getting to know a young man that one of the girls in the congregation had brought to church, and she could see sides of his personality that were hidden from the girl he was dating. But when my friend discussed this with the girl, she became angry instead of welcoming the wisdom and protection of an older woman (who later had her negative suspicions about the man confirmed). Don't be like that! Young women who welcome helpful evaluation and take it seriously rarely regret their decisions.

The preaching of the Word is the most vital way your local congregation helps you. If your pastor is faithfully expounding the Bible each Sunday, you need to be there to listen and grow. As you deepen in your understanding of the Word, use that as your standard: Scripture is the ultimate marriage guide and measure.

When you do find a mature believer or believing couple who will be able to help you through this process, tell them your thoughts. If they don't know you well, let them know about any past or present relationships, and what you hope the future holds. Read this book together, using the thoughts as starting points for discussion and application to your own situation. A mentor can help you apply biblical directives and principles to your individual situation. If you have the resources, invest in the books listed in the bibliography and go through them as well; you can use them your whole life.

If a young man wants to pursue or is pursuing a relationship with you now, specifically talk with your parents or mentors about how he will likely impact your life. God has given you the means of preaching and Christian fellowship for your protection: this book is simply a supplement and springboard to these good gifts! Go through the study questions with a mature believer who loves you and can help you cast a vision for a godly marriage for you. If you are not in a relationship with anyone, you can still discuss these issues to prepare for a possible marriage. We just have to be careful that we don't build up an idea of a perfect man in our heads—he isn't out there!

When we are in fellowship with God's people and accepting their help, we need to beware of another trap. When we are evaluating men, it's easy to behave as if we're shopping. It's easy to criticize and judge and sometimes forget that the person whom we are considering is a human being made in the image of God. The task we're engaged in is not like looking for shoes, trying them on for size and deciding if we can deal with the number of blisters that they will give us. We are looking at fellow creatures. If we are looking at Christian men (and we have to!), then we are looking at someone whom God loved from eternity. You are going to marry another sinner, so you can't look for perfection; look for patterns of sanctification and sin so that you can discern a trajectory.

In light of this, please use this book humbly, counting others as more worthy than yourself. This does not mean that we lower the standard for a husband; it means that we consider every other believer as more valuable to the Kingdom than we are, whether or not we end up marrying them. This happens when we can follow Paul in admitting that we are the worst of sinners (1 Tim. 1:15). That is hard to do, especially when we are evaluating someone! But God gives grace to the humble (James 4:6); so humble yourself in prayer before the Lord, asking Him to give you a spirit of gracious humility. Ask your parents, pastor, or mentor to keep you from gossiping, slandering, or belittling the very man whom you are considering. Also, as you prayerfully evaluate the person before you, or simply think about what is important in a future spouse, keep in mind that the man in question should also be going through a parallel process in evaluating you: prayerfully consider how your own life does or does not reflect biblical values of womanhood and wifehood.

So, I encourage you to use this book as a springboard to think about your own life, to evaluate where you are at and what sort of a person you are considering. In addition, ask people who know and love you for their input. Even if you don't agree with them (and you had better have good reason!), their observations will help you think through the issues and gain wisdom. Most of all, pray about these things; the cattle on a thousand hills belong to the Lord (Ps. 50:10) and so do all the men! If you are a child of God, He will ensure that all things are subservient to your salvation and growth in grace (Heidelberg Catechism Q&A 1). Godly marriages bring glory to God; He loves to provide for them and bless them. Ask the Creator of marriage to provide for you in this realm. 'Many a man proclaims his own steadfast love, but a faithful man who can find?' (Prov. 20:6). Pray that the Lord would give you a faithful man who loves Christ most and so can love you best.

2

Marriage will impact you spiritually

If you read only one chapter in this book, this is the one to read. The other ones, while not unimportant, are secondary compared with the weight that the spiritual element carries in a marriage.

Only in the Lord
The first principle that I would like to share with you is simple and direct: if the guy that you're thinking of is not a believer, you should stop dating him right now! Even if he seems open to change, it is never appropriate to yoke a redeemed soul with an unregenerate one—not even if you're 'only dating'. Christ has bought you with a price and it is simply not an option to give away that blood-bought heart

to someone who doesn't know and love your Lord. Doing so will cripple your spiritual development, open up a host of temptations, stifle your prayer life, make regular church going difficult, and cause massive parenting conflict if you have children. The idea that he is your soul-mate is a lie; his soul is a stranger to the grace that has saved you. Scripture tells you to walk away from his advances.

Many people find this point of view offensive and exclusivist. Why does the other person *have* to have the same beliefs as you? Inter-religious relationships are becoming the norm in Europe and North America, so these discussions are important. Perhaps some of this question comes from a misunderstanding: it can sound as though I am saying that I have the authority as a human being to reject other human beings. Now in one sense, that is true; nobody should be forced to marry anybody, but should have the freedom to reject any potential spouse. But as an individual, I do not have the authority to advise others to turn away from a potential spouse on the grounds of personal belief.

This is not merely personal belief, though. It is the Bible's clear teaching to those who profess the name of Christ. Not only in places such as 2 Corinthians 6:14, where we see clear directions against marrying someone of a different religion, but also throughout the Old and New Testaments, we see again and again the difficulties, problems, and even judgments that come from marrying someone with other beliefs. God takes it very seriously, calling it faithlessness to Him (Ezra 9). A person who holds to another or no religion has different moral standards, different family structures, and different religious expectations, which trickle into the way everyday life runs. Practical issues such as parenting, spending money, and entertainment are all common expressions of worldviews that are different and, at vital points, antithetical, because they have different gods, different holy books, and different goals for life and eternity. Often, in the emotional romance of a relationship, it is difficult to remember this.

'Christianity,' Martyn Lloyd-Jones writes, 'has something to say about the whole of our life. There is no aspect of life which it does not consider, which it does not govern. There must be no compartments in our Christian life.' When you date or marry someone who is not a Christian, you are assuming that you can compartmentalize that area of your life and treat it as outside the realm of religious influence; this ignores Scripture's clear directive to not be unequally yoked with an unbeliever (2 Cor. 6:14). When we choose to date or marry an unbeliever, we say that our attempts to grow closer to God are better than what He has commanded for our holiness. Your actions in your love-life will reveal whether or not you take Scripture and the God of Scripture seriously, or if your own wishes or rationale or feelings will come first.

We do not have the authority (even if we think we do) to determine what is right for us in regards to parameters for potential spouses, because we did not create marriage and can't simply design it in the way that seems best to us. God did, so His authority is final and binding. He created it to be a picture of Christ and the Church—no unbelieving guy will be able to even begin to approach that pattern.

If we are believers, then God's directives are for our own good. If He did not spare His own Son, will He not also give us every good thing (Rom. 8:32)? If a man is not a Christian, then the Bible says you may not marry him, not because God wants to keep something good from you, but because He wants to keep you from something harmful. Your Creator and Redeemer has your best interests in mind. His primary concern is not if the fellow is cute, or seems to understand and appreciate you, but if the man will bless your soul in the ways that only another follower of Christ can.

The soul is the most valuable part of the human being, which is why religion is such a massive aspect to consider in a relationship. Your soul is who you are at essence. It is eternal. If you are a Christian, your first relationship is with Christ, who has loved you with an everlasting love. He has brought you from death to life, from darkness to light, from rebellion to new obedience, all by grace. A man who does not know and love your Savior cannot really love you—especially your soul. He might *say* that he does, which really just shows that he does not understand at all. He might say that he is interested in Christianity: let your pastor explain it to him. Do not endanger your soul when there are others around to care for his—and there are. Ask your pastor and other godly men to step in and build relationships with him in place of you. Deciding not to date someone does not mean that you don't care for that person or desire him to grow spiritually; it just means that you recognize the truth of God's Word and are following His guidance in this area. God desires us to nurture others' spiritual lives, but caring for a person's spiritual development is not the same as consenting to date or even marry someone with whom you would be 'unequally yoked'.

Some people argue that marriage to an unbeliever has forced them to rely on God more: made them pray more, enabled them to witness more, made them value the church more. If someone was converted after marriage, that may be true. But when a professing believer knowingly marries an unbeliever, it is like a child stealing cookies, then protesting that they have a better appreciation for their mother's baking. It is true: they might appreciate her skills more, just as a Christian married to a non-Christian might pray more. But no mother will be pacified with such an excuse. God tells us plainly in His Word that what He loves most is obedience to His Word (1 Sam. 15:22; see also Exod. 23:22; Deut. 13:4; 30:16; Jer. 7:23; Ezek. 36:27; Rom. 6:16; Heb. 5:9). Obedience is how we show that we love Him (John 14:15; 1 John 5:2). God tells us just as plainly in that Word that we are to have no fellowship with darkness (2 Cor. 6:14). Knowingly choosing an unbelieving guy is disobedience: deliberate, decided sin. That in itself puts your soul in danger. Sin and misery go hand-in-hand.

A man who does not know Christ cannot be a Christ-like figure, loving you as Christ loved the Church as God calls him to in Ephesians 5. Pastor Jason Helopoulos warns single women about un-believing men: 'They will not be united with you on the most important thing, which shapes every-thing else, and yet you will be united in one flesh. As I have sat with grieving Christians, struggling to know how to live in a godless marriage, I hear in their cries the reality that there are few things more lonely than knowing that the person you are the closest to in this life is far from you in almost every way. If you don't have Christ in common, it is hard to have much in common.' Do not knowingly submit yourself to a false head (Eph. 5:23).

Of the same mind

If you are already confident that the guy who interests you *is* a believer, how can you further assess your spiritual 'fit'? A good place to start is by asking if your theological views are similar. Marrying someone from a different denomination might seem like a minor detail compared to marrying a Muslim or atheist. But while it may be better, it certainly isn't minor. My father made sure that my sister and I were married to men who had very similar theology to ours. He wasn't being restrictive or narrow: he was saving us from a lifetime of conflict. Think about all of the possible points of conflict with a Christian husband who has different theology from you: what church to go to, whether or not to baptize children, what is modest clothing, how to celebrate Christmas, how to discipline children, whether or not to drink alcohol, what music to listen to, etc. The list is as large as your differences. This does not mean that you have to have identical views (or simply adopt all of his) on every issue. What it does mean is that the major issues need to be sorted out, preferably with the help of a discerning parent or pastor. My brother-in-law fell in love with a Christian with different beliefs about baptism: they spent many hours talking, reading, praying and even crying over the issue until they reached the point where they held the same position. Then they got engaged. All of those hours invested up front saved them months and years of married struggle. If they had not been able to come to agreement or respect each other during the discussion process, that would have been a sign that long-term partnership was not a realistic or wise option.

Is the fellow of whom you are thinking a spiritual leader? A husband, John Angell James says, 'is to be the prophet, priest, and king of the family, to instruct their minds, to lead their devotions ... the wife is to be of one mind with him.' The ability to lead spiritually is important, and a large part of it includes shouldering the burden of ensuring that all members of the family are having personal devotions, leading family worship, and attending to his own spiritual life in order to be able to do these things.

The ability to lead in and of itself is not a green light. History is filled with leaders (in and out of the home) who led their followers into sin and misery. But the willingness and ability to take the spiritual initiative as head of the family is essential in a husband. This comes to some men naturally, while others have to learn it. Just because the man whom you're thinking of does not fully exhibit this trait does not mean that he never will. If everything else is as it should be, developing this should be relatively simple with the help of a pastor and godly mentor. But it's essential to see him exhibiting it *before* you say 'I do.'

There has been some push back against this idea recently. Some Christians argue that the attribute of spiritual leadership marked by initiating personal and family worship is a wrongly stereotyped 'masculine' quality. They say that men with 'traditionally feminine' gifts such as hospitality, patience, encouragement or service are just as spiritually developed and qualified to be husbands.

But the head of a home, just like the head of a nation, needs to have certain qualities that followers do not. A love for America and doing good things for fellow Americans does not qualify someone for the presidency. A president needs to be able to lead: to make decisions, give speeches, understand policy, direct the military. Similarly, a husband needs to be able to lead: to pray with and for the family; teach them the Word; make spiritual decisions with his wife's help; direct the spiritual growth of the children. While a lack of spiritual leadership does not mean that someone is not fit to be a Christian man, it does mean that he is not a strong model of what a Christian husband and father, should be, at least not yet. Such men can serve on committees, not lead wives and children. And I dare say that the man who is a true spiritual leader will be growing in the other spiritual gifts as well; true spiritual leaders are also patient and encouraging and willing to serve.

If a man is a spiritual leader, he is going to make spiritual growth a priority; other things will come after. Will your future husband lead you in prayer, Bible reading, family devotions, and public worship? Will he help you work the family schedule around these staples? Or will you be on your own, trying to fit them in where you can? One of the early and big indicators to me that my (then) boyfriend would be a strong spiritual leader was that at the end of our second date, he pulled out a Bible and said that he would like to make a habit of reading a chapter and praying together each time he brought me home from a night out. More than a decade of marriage later, it is still a solid habit—now every night as well as dates! My husband's mentors and Christian friends have varying patterns of spiritually leading their wives, but they all involve daily prayer for their wife and reading Scripture together, either when the alarm goes off, after a meal, or before the lights go out at the end of the day. Can you see your boyfriend keeping that sort of commitment to having the Word at the center of your relationship for your growth?

How will you make decisions such as where to worship, or what to allow the kids to watch/read/listen to? Do you respect his spiritual integrity and leadership so much that you can submit to his decisions after you have discussed the issue together (1 Pet. 3:6)? If not, be prepared for a contentious, unhappy home, where you are struggling to have your own way at the cost of your relationship. If you are prepared to submit to a biblical decision, God will bless that obedience with domestic peace (Ps. 128:3-4; 133).

Loving leadership

What about your sins and shortcomings? English theologian John Owen reminds us, 'The vigor and power of our spiritual life depend on our mortification (of sin).' Do you want an energetic spiritual life? Do you want comfort and peace in your soul? Then marry a man who loves you enough to lovingly point out areas where you need to kill sin. Marry a man who knows how to fight temptation and can help you fight it. Marry a man who can forgive you when you sin against him, as you most certainly will. Marry someone mature enough to deal with conflict graciously and forgive as they have been forgiven by Christ. There are many weak husbands out there who do not have the gumption to take their wives aside and out of love for their souls point out patterns of sin. Intimacy with a man who cannot or will not do this will allow you to become hardened in your own besetting sins. But a man who *will* do this is preparing your soul for glory throughout your marriage.

Of course, the method that a husband uses will partly depend on his personality. If he is a godly man, correction will always be done out of love and with love. You can imagine that, at times, the reformer Martin Luther complained about Katie's sometimes-sharp tongue. Katie could handle that sort of pressure as she knew it came out of Martin's love for her soul, which he loved more than domestic peace. Are you convinced that the man you will marry has your spiritual good first on his heart, even above your feelings?

Is the man who is pursuing you open about his own spiritual life, or will you always be guessing what is going on in his soul? You cannot encourage and support a man when you don't know what he is discouraged about or where he is weakening. Baptist missionary Adoniram Judson was very open with Ann about his spiritual condition; this allowed his wife to be a helpmeet to him in this vital area. Marry a man who is open about the state of his soul with the people to whom he is closest.

Is the man who is pursuing you willing to listen to how it is going with your soul? Is he going to ask you about your spiritual health, growth in prayer, and communion with God, or will he leave that to your pastor? If he tends to leave these kinds of issues to others, that's a symptom of his own spiritual immaturity and is another warning sign.

Is he going to lead the children in spiritual matters, or will you have to spearhead that? In church, is he going to help the kids sit well, pray, and find the hymn, or will you be the one pointing out what is happening next and helping the family keep up? Many women have married spiritually immature men, thinking that it wasn't a big issue for the kids, or that the man would change when he became a father. They were wrong. They bear the scars, and so do their children. Spiritually slack fathers almost never produce spiritually mature sons. Ultimately, it is God who converts and sanctifies; fathers can either hinder or facilitate the Spirit's work in their children's lives.

But the reverse is also true: a man dedicated to the spiritual education and development of the children often sees godly children growing up to take his place in the community and Kingdom. God blesses the use of ordained means to save covenant children. Jonathan Edwards and his children are almost proverbial as examples. While Edwards was very absent-minded in much of life, a deliberate, concentrated teaching of the living Word in the home bore generations of fruit in his family. That gospel-centered home and its inheritors produced 100 ministers, in addition to hundreds of doctors, professors, lawyers, authors, and other public servants. Will your future husband be dedicated to this and will he have your help and support? Intimacy with a man who will do little for the children's spiritual health will make your efforts even more difficult than they naturally are.

But intimacy with a man who pursues this goal will mean that you can work as parenting partners nurturing covenant children. One large aspect of Christian marriage, Edmund Spenser said, is for a husband and wife to work 'Of blessed Saints for to increase the count.' This is what Malachi 2:15 tells us: one of the reasons God instituted marriage was so that children would have a place to grow up surrounded by biblical teaching. 'Did he not make them one, with a portion of the Spirit in their union?' the prophet asks. 'And what was the one God seeking? Godly offspring.' That is why it is important to marry someone who is excited about raising children in the fear and admonition of the Lord, teaching them the joy of salvation.

If the fellow of whom you are thinking is a strong, growing believer who is willing to care for you spiritually, then you have a soul-mate. That does not mean that you have to marry him; it does mean that you already have the most essential and important aspects of a healthy marriage lined up. Since your souls are both in Christ and both growing in grace, they are compatible, even if there are bugs to work out (and there are). If you can achieve more for the Lord as a married couple than as individuals, there is strong incentive to marriage. If the man is not a strong believer and especially if he is regressing in his piety, watch out: the health of your eternity is at stake. As you follow Christ in all other areas of life, follow Him with respect to your love life as well, acknowledging that His care for you far exceeds that of any earthly partner; it is much better to walk with Christ as a single person than to depart from Him while married.

As a believer, your salvation is secure in Christ, but the judgment you receive on the Last Day will be greatly impacted by your spouse (1 Cor. 3:12-15). A husband will either enable and encourage you to be spiritually fruitful, or stunt your growth. John Angell James urged single people to secure a spouse 'who will be a helpmate for him in reference to another world ... The highest end of the connubial state is lost, if it be not rendered helpful to our piety, and yet this end is too generally neglected.' The most important role of marriage is to prepare you for eternity, though it is easy to ignore or belittle this aspect while focusing on present pressures and opportunities. For this reason, I encourage you to think carefully about the eternal dimensions of your potential partnership.

3

Marriage will impact you emotionally

Men tend to stereotype us as emotional creatures, don't they? Well, it's not all their fault. There's good reason to think this. When is the last time you saw a guy crying in the church foyer as his friends patted his back? Ever known a fellow who was irritable a certain time of the month? Or a man who felt snubbed by a comment about his clothes and had to work through the situation with his dad? Like I said, stereotypes are not all the guys' fault. We do tend to express our emotions differently from men, so it is important to think through some of the impact that intimacy with a less emotionally expressive person—a husband!—can have on you.

How does your potential spouse respond to your emotional ups and downs? Is the guy you're thinking of going to encourage you, love you, be kind to you, and seek to understand you, or will he want to go out with the guys when you're having a hard night? Will he listen when you are struggling with something, or will he be preoccupied with a video game? Is he going to be annoyed when you cry, or will he get you Kleenex and give you a hug? Is he going to understand that you are probably more tender than he is, more sensitive to issues and comments, or is he regularly going to run roughshod over your feelings?

This is not to say that a man should be expected to feel everything that we do. We have to get rid of princess complexes, but we do have emotional needs. Any guy who is uncaring about your feelings and self-esteem is selfish and should be left alone. Intimacy with such a man will leave you feeling alone and unprotected. One woman I know of was struggling to breastfeed, believing that that was the best thing for her baby, but it was very difficult. Instead of giving support and encouragement, the husband would make mooing sounds whenever he saw his wife working at it! That kind of response is worse than simply failing to understand or relate to his wife's experience; this husband was actively discouraging her from something that she deemed important. Understanding how a man will respond to your emotional make-up is vital to preparing for marriage.

Intimacy with a man who encourages you in your calling and is willing to put down his work and help you sort through an issue will create security and emotional safety. When you know that your fears and problems won't be laughed at or shrugged off or ignored, it creates an environment of safety—you can open your emotional life up to your husband knowing that you will find help, comfort, encouragement, or a shared sorrow, excitement, or surprise. This sort of protection is such a joy for a wife, not only because it is a safe haven, but also because it fosters further intimacy.

Have you ever seen a woman who was always insecure despite being perfectly normal? This can often be traced back to a belittling father or husband—men who are rough and demeaning in the way they treat women. Women who are generally comfortable with themselves usually have secure emotional relationships with their fathers and husbands; they have a protected, safe place to run to when they feel vulnerable. Their husbands and fathers respect their personhood and personal needs. The strength of an emotional bond in marriage helps make women stronger. Is that what will happen in marriage with the man you have in mind? How do you know, or what makes you wonder?

Often, it is a man's speech that will either emotionally build up or tear down his wife. Boyfriends rarely speak in demeaning or rough ways to their girlfriends (if he does, consider that a strong reason to get away now!). If you are looking for a way to see how he will speak to you after years of living under the same roof, listen to him talk with his mother. Men who disrespect, belittle, ignore, or abuse their mothers in conversation will almost always do the same thing to their wives. Pay careful attention to this indicator; his mother has endured this demeaning behavior for years. Don't lock yourself in for life. You may also want to attend to how he speaks to other relatives, especially women. All families have difficult dynamics and sources of frustration, so this is not to say that he never critiques or complains about his family. But it is to say that the way that he interacts with them should model biblical principles of communication and speaking in love. Even the way he speaks to waiters and other service people will reveal his trajectory in this area.

There are couples (about ten percent, according to statistics[1]) who are never able to have children. If you discover that you are one of them, is your husband going to be frustrated with you? Blame you? Ignore what a grief that it is to you? Or will he gently shepherd you through this deep emotional valley? What about the difficult circumstances of

---

1   http://www.cdc.gov/nchs/fastats/fertile.htm

losing a grandparent, parent, or loved one to death? This person will walk with you through all of the major life events that are to come, and his ability to nurture and care for you is an important component of his suitability as a spouse.

When you are struggling with negative feelings, will that man be ready to find out what you are afraid of so that he can protect you, ask (or note) what makes you feel ugly and tell you that you that you're wrong, understand why you are discouraged and point you to the cross? Will he be happy when you are, even if he doesn't get why; laugh at something that strikes you as hilarious because he shares your joy? Will he bring thanksgiving before God in prayer when he sees that you have been blessed even if he was not? Or will he turn in and become emotionally closed towards you?

The issue is not whether your boyfriend understands you perfectly, anticipating and responding to your emotional state in exactly the right way. The issue is whether he wants to understand and shepherd you in this area. There is a difference between his not realizing how you feel, and his ignoring you when you communicate how you feel. There is also a difference between his being a little frustrated when he tries to figure you out, and his rejecting you or refusing any support when he does not understand. Effort and clear communication are key: a loving husband will try to listen, then try and respond in a biblically helpful way. Is your boyfriend on a good trajectory here?

Scripture calls every believer to rejoice with rejoicing Christians and to mourn with grieving Christians (Rom. 12:15). This should be even more true of a husband and wife. A man who cannot share in your emotional life and be a positive influence on it isn't ready to ask you to marry him; he still needs to learn the basics of Christian fellowship! A husband can cripple or foster emotional health, so take care in this area—pay attention to how his emotions and yours intertwine.

4

Marriage will impact you mentally

Do you know a couple who finish each other's sentences? Maybe they even know what the other is thinking before they say it. The husband walks into the room and says, 'Honey, did—' and she answers right away, 'Yeah, I called and it's fine,' and he says, 'Good—thanks!' What went on there? Nobody else understands what is going on, but the two people are so aware of each other's thoughts and thought patterns that they know what the other person is dealing with mentally, even when it is a small thing. This has developed over time, through clear communication, a respect for the other person, and common goals.

The importance of personhood

This intimacy doesn't come about because the husband and wife are constantly nagging each other about what the other person is thinking or feeling. The intimacy that marriage brings should not violate the personhood of either spouse. You are first and foremost a human being made in the image of God and, if you are a Christian, one who is redeemed. That is your primary relationship, one that involves the deepest intimacy. You are first a redeemed human being, then a wife. A husband has no right to violate your personhood by demanding to know everything about you, just as you have no right to violate his that way. There are some things, though they are rare, that a husband has no right to know— only your Creator and God does. Of course, openness and free communication in a marriage are part of what forms the deep trust and respect that are necessary for a healthy relationship. Spiritual, emotional, intellectual and relational honesty are essential.

But there are parts of your person that only God has a right to know—issues or experiences that you cannot communicate because they would be too great a burden to your spouse, too complex for you to communicate, or too subtle for you to even understand. Where there is an atmosphere of openness and trust through frequent and personal communication, it is neither necessary nor legitimate for a husband to dig and dig for every detail of your past experiences, spiritual routines, or physical condition. In a healthy marriage, a husband will have or earn the confidence of his wife, who will love to tell him everything that she feels the need to share. A husband who tries to extract these sorts of things from a wife and attempts to have total knowledge about and over her is behaving more like a tyrant than a fellow creature whose job is to tenderly lead her. Husbands aren't made to be omniscient. They are made to lead and love wives who trust them. That is how intimacy develops in this area.

Protecting your mind

One way of thinking about how your potential future husband will engage with you in this way is to ask, is he going to encourage my intellectual development, or will he neglect it? I am blessed to have a husband who is always bringing books home, directing me to online articles, and discussing issues, partly because he sees my intellectual growth as part of his job description as a husband. He recognizes that God made me with a brain and that staying at home with small children sometimes cramps my mental muscles. And so he responds by providing mental recreation that develops my mind. Not all wives like an armful of books unloaded at them right before supper, but all wives have minds that need to be cared for and developed. How will your boyfriend do that for you in the future?

Another important question is, will he value your opinions and listen to what you are thinking, or will he disregard your thoughts? There are husbands out there who do not allow their wives to hold a different opinion from the one they do on anything. Certainly, there are issues where differing opinions can ruin a marriage: who God is, how to handle money, raise children, and many more would all count as issues where harmony is vital for a successful relationship. But other issues are secondary. Will the man who you are thinking of be upset or controlling if you want to hold different opinions? Is he comfortable discussing the issues that you do not agree on in a gracious and helpful way? This does not mean that there is never conflict or concern—each of us holds our views closely, and occasional 'upsets' around key issues might be normal. But marriage to a man who respects you on a mental and intellectual level and agrees with you on the basics means that disagreements do not turn into major conflicts. It also means that one person's point of view is not consistently disregarded or discounted. One multi-month discussion in our home was on the origin of the soul: how the soul of a baby *in utero* comes to exist. I hold one position, and my husband holds another (both positions,

I might add, are orthodox!). We discussed and asked theologians (living and dead) for their input, and added to our arguments, more for fun than for anything else. While we are each convinced of our own position, the discussion does not change how we parent or view God or salvation since there is nothing we can do about it anyway. We can talk about it without anger or irritation; our discussion on this point is simply a point of difference that has very little bearing on our lives together.

Having a husband do all the thinking and form all the opinions for a family is a dangerous thing. For one thing, it wastes the wife's God-given mental abilities. But it also means that it is easier for the husband to form errant or unbalanced opinions. Discussing issues with a godly wife has saved many men from foolish ideas and actions. Does your man understand this?

Is he going to help you manage stress so that your mind is not burdened that way, or is he going to let you struggle through issues alone? Is he going to care for you and be thoughtful of you if you are experiencing mental strain, or will he ignore it? I know of a woman who could handle pregnancy and child birth very well physically, but postpartum depression took a huge toll on her mind. The husband overlooked it, continuing to have more children, until his wife ended up in a mental institution. That is mental abuse, not loving leadership.

Thinking through personality and work

What about your respective outlooks on how you handle what matters? Some people are 'micro,' noticing every detail and obsessing about getting it right. Others are 'macro,' seeing the big picture and going for the goal with less regard for exactly how they get there. A husband and wife of different temperaments can work together, covering each other's weaknesses, but it is a helpful thing to think through and understand ahead of time. Is the man that is interested in you going to get irritated or blow up or obsess over every little thing? Are genuine accidents and mistakes going to send him off in a fit of anger each time, so that you are afraid of his partnership in something? Or will he be pursuing goals in ways that trouble you? In either case, the husband's habits can place unnecessary mental stress on the wife. That should not be. A husband and wife should be able to complement each other in this area; if your boyfriend is a 'micro' person, does he have the maturity to handle it when you don't get details right (or don't get them at all!)? If he is a 'macro' type, does he have the sensitivity and honesty to pursue a goal considering others and being careful not to make an idol out of it?

Encouragement is a huge part of a husband's job in caring for his wife's mental health. It is an expression of his recognition that your work in all spheres of life is valuable and that you are working hard at it. This is especially true for women who are staying in the home to care for the children: you have no boss to tell you that you're doing well, no annual review, no salary raise. In other words, you spend most of your week doing unpaid, physical work in a house with crazy little people who sometimes seem bent on making you crazy. If a husband cannot remind you that this work is vital, then that is a problem. If a man cannot come home at the end of the day and tell you that you are doing a good job or very lovingly encourage you to do a little better, being a wife and mother will grow old quickly, and you will not be able to persist as confidently as if you had his support. If a husband – the person at the core of your life – is not there to encourage you in your life's work, you may begin to think that it is unimportant. Does your boyfriend see value in what you are doing or hope to do? Then you will likely have the mental stamina to push through. One way that you and he can work together is by supporting each other in your respective callings and daily activities.

One other way a husband can wear down his wife mentally is by having unrealistic views of himself, usually expressed by thinking and talking too much about himself. If your boyfriend is always communicating how gifted, able, intelligent, hard-working, tired, sick, or muscular he is, watch out! That gets old fast, and it is demeaning to live with someone whose opinion of himself does not correspond to reality and reveals self-centeredness. A need for either frequent affirmation or admiration can make a wife feel patronized, minimized, or overlooked by the man who should be humbly serving as he dies to self.

You might think that the intellectual or mental side of a marriage is small. It's bigger than you think. Consider it seriously.

5

Marriage will impact you physically

'Likewise, husbands, live with your wives in an understanding way, showing honor to the woman as the weaker vessel, since they are heirs with you of the grace of life, so that your prayers may not be hindered.' I did not come up with the idea that women are weaker than men: the Bible tells us so (1 Pet. 3:7). And since God is the One who made us, He has the authority to tell us so. We might not like to admit it, and feminists may shout in protest at it, but deep down, we know it is true. Even the politically correct American military recognizes this, placing lighter demands for enlisted women's physical qualifications than it does for men. In general, women are physically weaker than men.

But what does that have to do with marriage? Why does a woman's weaker—not lesser—physical make-up matter in a romantic relationship? It matters because in this one-flesh relationship, the burden of providing and protecting falls on the husband. Men are told to 'love their wives as their own bodies,' because, 'he who loves his wife loves himself. For no one ever hated his own flesh, but nourishes and cherishes it, just as Christ does the church' (Eph. 5:28-29). Since we are weaker vessels to be nourished and cared for, we need to be thinking about boyfriends' attitudes in this area, too.

The basics of provision

Does your boyfriend understand that your body is of worth because God made it, claimed it as His along with your soul when He saved you, and will return from Heaven to raise your body in glory? A man who has a biblical understanding of the body will have the understanding that he needs in order to care for and lead you in this area.

A man who does not provide for his household, 1 Timothy 5:8 tells us, 'has denied the faith and is worse than an unbeliever.' Is the guy you're with going to provide for your basic needs? Will he be able to shelter, clothe, and feed you? At one point in our marriage, I was worried that there was no employment opportunity. My husband assured me that he would work at McDonalds, dig ditches, clean up road-kill—whatever it took to provide for the family, regardless of his gifts and training. That's the kind of attitude you want. You might have to help ease the financial burden, but unless your husband is disabled or there is another unusual circumstance, you shouldn't have to carry it yourself. A husband should be committed to providing for his wife.

The money which comes into a marriage can affect its physical, creature-comfort quality. It can also be a source of tension. Regardless of the amount of money you have, it should be something that is freely shared between husband and wife. *The Book of Common Prayer*, in the marriage service, has the bride and bridegroom vow that they will endow the other with 'all my worldly goods'. There are couples who have separate bank accounts. This can be done well, freely sharing pins, other information, and funds, or it can be done badly, creating an economic divide where there should be oneness.

The other extreme is to have one spouse controlling all the money. That is equally devastating to full intimacy because it demonstrates a love of money, a lack of trust, or both. One wife that I know had to go to her husband whenever the family needed groceries. He controlled the finances to the point that she had to ask him for the amount of money that she would need to buy food for the week. Any change had to be returned to him. This kind of posture demeans a wife; she is being treated like a suspect servant, not a cherished helpmeet. Can you see something like that happening in your relationship?

Will the man who is interested in you be willing to sacrifice 'extras' in order to provide for children? Will unnecessary amusements chip away at savings or even a basic budget, creating debt? What are his financial priorities? Does giving to the church excite and motivate him? Is he sacrificial within his means, giving to those in need? Or is he miserly, obsessively hoarding in unreasonable thrift?

A husband should be willing and able to work hard to provide for his family and serve the church. What is your boyfriend's work ethic like? Is he a workaholic who idolizes his job and productivity? That will take its toll on your marriage and discredit his Christian profession, as wife and children become career casualties. But in some ways, a sluggard is worse; a wife and children are just as neglected, but without the physical provision that work brings. Being a husband and father is hard work. What is your boyfriend's attitude toward his job? Does he work hard at it, giving it his best to God's glory? Have you seen him pitch in with work at church or the community to understand what his work ethic looks like? It's something you should know before you walk down the aisle.

The dangers of abuse

Will the man you are with care for your body or abuse it? One way to gauge this is to look at how he relates to you physically now. Does he ever respond to your words or actions with anything but kind physical contact? Does he ever take out anger or frustration in violence, even on furniture or walls? If he gives you little smacks, kicks, etc. when you're dating, get away. If he is willing to do this when you are dating and he is supposed to be winning your heart, he is almost guaranteed to escalate his mistreatment of you or shift his abuse to you after you are married. Statistics show that's especially true when you are pregnant. Is he going to care for and protect your body, or will he hurt it? There are women in churches across America who thought that it was no big deal to get little (sort of friendly) punches or slaps from their boyfriends from time to time while dating, but who are now covering up the bruises from their husbands.

But this is not the only physical abuse possible. Too much hard work can also damage a wife's body. A man who expects a wife to do all the cleaning, all the child care, all the gardening, all the shopping, all the house repairs, all the banking, all the everything, is treating her like a slave, not a wife. Hard work at the office is no excuse for such treatment at home. Adequate sleep, rest, and help are all things that a husband needs to provide for a wife, where possible. Do not marry someone who thinks that doing the dishes now and then is degrading for a man. Do not marry someone who will not recognize when you are overburdened with things and need a break.

What about maintaining physical health? Will the man who is interested in you encourage and facilitate healthy eating and exercise so that you can maintain good health? That is the middle ground between obsessing over how a wife looks and what she eats on one hand, forcing her to go beyond reasonable measures, and neglecting her physical health on the other. One indicator of how a guy will behave in this area is how he cares for his own body now. Does he pursue looks or health, or are neither on his radar? A biblical view of the body and a Christian's responsibility to maintain the 'tent' that God gave us (2 Cor. 5:1, 4); a lack of this understanding is something that will have daily implications.

Another question to consider is, will your husband protect you from other physical harm if it arises? Is he the sort of fellow who will put himself between you and an intruder if your home is broken into? Or will he be trying to climb out the window? In one church we were part of, a dating couple arrived for the service—the fellow with broken ribs. They had been walking in a downtown area when a driver lost control of a vehicle that headed right towards the couple at a high speed. The man no-ticed, pushed his girlfriend out of the car's path, then belly-flopped on the sidewalk. She was fine; he was too, eventually. They became engaged shortly after. Chivalry and physical protection are not the stuff of fairy tales. Every wife is entitled to whatever physical safety her husband can reasonably provide. Does your boyfriend think that's old-fashioned?

Sexual fidelity

Marriage will also affect you sexually. Because the world talks so much about sex, some Christians think that it is inappropriate for believers to discuss. Chastity, refraining from sex until marriage and then engaging in it only in marriage, is of course what Scripture calls us to. But because our culture speaks so often and so confusedly about sex, we have to talk about it, including before and outside of marriage. The Bible itself talks about sex quite a bit, so it's not something we can shy away from or ignore. It is necessary for Christians to have a god-ly view of the sexuality that God gave them, and you can't create that perspective with a snap of the fingers; it is something that is developed with care over time. The marriage bed is sacred and private, but the worldview in which it fits needs to be ham-mered out before the wedding night. Sadly, many men who seem like good, Christian guys in other areas are stunted or deformed in their views of sex. You need to discuss this aspect of marriage with your boyfriend before you are married, preferably with a wise, married Christian couple, in order to discern how a marriage will form this area of your life. This is especially true for people who have had previous sexual experience.

Our culture often throws around the term, 'sexual incompatibility': a lack of 'chemistry' between sexual 'partners.' Scripture knows of no such incompatibility. In biblical terms, sexual compatibility comes when two healthy, married people of the opposite gender engage in sexual activity for the purpose of blessing their spouse, with thanks to God for this gift. If medical issues arise, they are not a sign of incompatibility, but of illness. Where there is a lack of 'chemistry,' it is almost always because of an underlying issue such as selfishness, lack of trust, past history, or another problem which needs to be addressed itself. The idea that we need to assess or test our sexual compatibility before marriage is a concept totally opposed to the Bible's view of married sexuality. Christians are not called to have amazing sex. They are called to serve in every area. Does your boyfriend understand this?

Will the man you are with honor the marriage bed in physical and mental faithfulness to you or will he flirt, have lots of close female friends, or even leave you for another woman? You can't always predict these issues, but if the seeds or practices are already there, that's a reason for real concern. I recently saw a newly married couple, and the husband was openly flirting with another woman. Unless something drastic happens, that marriage is headed for disaster. How each of you will handle relationships with people of the opposite gender is an important and sensitive topic that should be discussed and approached with mutual agreement as much as possible. If you don't feel comfortable with his actions or attitudes in this area, it's important to talk about that with him, and, if you cannot come to resolution, to recognize that a sound relationship cannot be built on a faulty foundation.

What about other aspects of sexual fidelity? Our culture is so saturated with pornography that few men are untouched by it, and many are addicted. Because of this, it is to be expected that your boyfriend should have accountability and protection in this area. One way of accomplishing this is for you (or a pastor) to ask your boyfriend about installing a filter on his computer. If he does struggle with pornography, suggest that he install software on his computer that tracks visited sites and e-mails the list to someone who would hold him accountable. Likewise, he could try to limit his Internet use to more public places. You may also want to encourage him to talk to his pastor or mentor about his struggles and experiences in this area. A man who refuses accountability or fails to acknowledge the serious threat of pornographic material is waving a huge red flag: take it seriously.

If you already know that your boyfriend is habitually or regularly viewing pornography, that is a strong reason to end the relationship. It is realistic, not perfectionistic, to expect a Christian man to have victory over this sin—*before* you lock yourself in for life. Here's why: A man who is a Christian has the power of the Holy Spirit and so can fight against sin, even strong sin, and win. An addiction to pornography is very serious because it reveals that the person allowing that addiction is fundamentally selfish and unloving. He does not care that the woman on the screen is a victim, and that as a human being who bears God's image, she is being violated by evil men. The man with a porn addiction does not care that the real woman he claims to love is damaged by his behavior, which not only creates emotional barriers but also unrealistic physical expectations. That man loves women for what they can give him physically, instead of as persons made in the image of God. Pornography cultivates adulterous pleasures instead of the pleasures of God-ordained marriage and communion with Himself. It violates what God has deemed to be good. The man who is addicted to porn can't see God's holiness, can't see God's image in others, can't see his own sinfulness. If a man persists in this sin over time, this is reason to call into question his salvation and certainly his suitability for marriage. He values porn more than he values Jesus: have nothing to do with him until he has, over months or years, developped a track record of real victory in this area.

Is he going to be tender and gentle to you in bed? Is sexual intimacy with this man going to bring your body pain, pushing past reasonable, natural limits? One indicator of this sort of selfishness will be clear now: is he pushing the bounds of chastity while you are single? If so, he is not doing so out of love for you, and this sort of pattern will continue into marriage unless grace intervenes. If he is respecting and guarding chastity now, that is an indicator of his selfless ability to care for the body of the woman he says he loves.

Does the man that you are thinking of have a biblical view of what normal, *married* sexuality is? Some men, even Christian ones, see nothing wrong with 'kinky' sex. Our culture is trying, with frightening success, to realign what is normal for sex, even for married couples. It is taking what belonged to the red light districts fifty years ago and making it mainstream. Do you know what your boyfriend thinks is 'normal' and what is informing that standard? Or are you going to be shocked and disgusted after the wedding? I know one young woman who told her fiancé that certain acts, stripping, and even lingerie were not going to be a part of their relationship: she would be a Protestant wife, not a prostitute. He agreed. This doesn't mean that *you* have to reject lingerie: it does mean that Christians are to reject all sexual deviance, even when expressed in a marriage. In her bestselling book, *Secret Thoughts of an Unlikely Convert*, Rosaria Butterfield states, 'Christians act as though marriage redeems sin. Marriage does not redeem sin; only Jesus himself can do that.' Will this reality play out in your sexual relationship? Does your boyfriend agree with you on these things? Do you both agree with Scripture, holding on to what is pure and good and beautiful in your sexual monogamy (Phil. 4:8; Eph. 5:3)?

What about family planning and birth control? Do you and your boyfriend share a biblical perspective on how to plan pregnancies in a way that obeys Genesis (1:28) and protects your body? Does he understand that being fruitful and multiplying does not mean that your physical limitations are ignored? How about the opposite: will he encourage or demand that you use birth control that has short- or long-term effects on your health? Does he honor the reality that life begins at conception? Does he take seriously the need to evaluate which birth-control methods are potentially abortive (by either preventing a fertilized egg from implanting or causing the death of an implanted embryo)? A man who loves you will seek to walk with biblical wisdom through these issues.

Most pregnant women need some extra help with cleaning, laundry, etc. If the Lord gives you pregnancy, will your then-husband understand this season of life and protect your body and the health of the baby by pitching in until you are recovered from delivery? Or will you be struggling through the pregnancy exhausted, taking months to recover? Look at how he treats you when you have a small illness, or watch his parents' interactions during an illness for a good indication of what is shaping his perspective here.

Your body needs care and protection. Beware of a man who does not understand this or fails to demonstrate his understanding in practice. Pray that God will provide you with a man who will care for you as for his own body (Eph. 5:28).

6

Marriage will impact you relationally

Family and community

How's your relationship with your mother? Your dad? Do you love them? Does your boyfriend? Fast forward ten years: you tell your husband that your mother is coming for the weekend. Is he excited? Disappointed? Angry? Making snide jokes with his friends? Of course, a husband should come first in your priority of relationships, as you both leave father and mother and cleave to one another. But parents are still a big part of the picture. Whatever negative feelings he has about your parents now will probably be amplified after marriage.

Abusive men often cut off relationships with in-laws and keep their wives away from parents, as fathers and mothers are often the first to pick up on bad vibes. While parents can unbiblically hold on to their daughters after marriage, they can also sense when something is wrong, and ungodly men don't like it. Your marriage will either strengthen or damage—even destroy—your relationship with your parents. The people who know you best and love you most right now could be cut out of the picture by a husband who hates them.

It's the same with sisters and friends. Will they be welcomed, at reasonable times, in your home? Will the guy who you're with encourage healthy relationships with other women, or will he be jealous of normal, biblical friendships? One wife told me that the first warning sign she saw in her adulterous ex-husband was that he was embarrassed by her normal interactions with other people. He pulled away from her when she tried to build healthy relationships with others. Stay away from men like that.

It's also useful to look at how he views his own family and whether or not he treats his family and yours similarly. It's normal for the behavior of in-laws to be off-putting at times, so it's no surprise if each of you has questions or concerns about the others' extended family. But if he rejects your family, while gravitating toward his own, or if he seems to have unrealistic expectations about your relationships with either your own family or his, then these are important warning signs about the future. Perhaps he comes from a broken family or is estranged from a parent or sibling, and there are traceable reasons for his difficulty in understanding what normal family relationships look like. That might not be a deal-breaker, but it is an aspect to consider and seek counsel about.

Will the man whom you are thinking of help you mentor younger women and be thankful when older women mentor you, or will he belittle that? I am so thankful for several pastors that we have had who have allowed or enabled their wives to mentor me. Mentoring someone takes time and thought. Will your future husband see this as part of your calling as laid out in Titus 2:4? Or will he demand that all of your time and thought be spent on him?

Have either of you considered the area of hospitality, and what role it will play in your relationship after marriage? Hospitality is one of Scripture's commands to Christians (Rom. 12:13; 1 Pet. 4:9), and is one of the major ways that we should be meeting strangers, getting to know them better, and strengthening ties with friends. If the man whom you are considering thinks of home as a place of isolation and is not interested in the idea of being a godly host, that is an issue that will keep you from obeying the Bible's clear directive in this area. It will also prevent you from forming and deepening relationships with others. This is not to say that there shouldn't be some weekends or 'down times' when just the two of you enjoy your home life together. But if he *never* wants to host others, this is a sign that something is awry.

Another relational dynamic to think about is this: if you have children, how will the man you're thinking of shape the way that you relate to them? Is he the sort of man who sees children as a bother, an accessory, or as a means to some sort of personal benefit? Or does he recognize that children are an inheritance from the Lord, to be welcomed into the family as precious gifts? A man who is not going to encourage and facilitate your sacrificial mothering will make your relationship with the children that much harder. The same is true for a man who does not teach the children to respect and honor you as he does. Children whose fathers teach them to rise up and call their mothers blessed usually have good relationships with those mothers.

Your other half

While all other relationships matter, some deeply, your relationship with your husband is the one that will shape you the most of any other relationship, simply because of the closeness of marriage. Are you looking forward to that shaping you? Do you look forward to living together, talking together, eating together, sleeping together, doing yard work together, paying bills together, as long as you both shall live? Or is he going to be going out with the guys every chance that he gets, like the straying bird that Solomon describes (Prov. 27:8)? Are you his best friend and is he excited that you are? If there is something about this man that makes you hesitate to live that closely with him, don't ignore it. Is your relationship with this person something that you want to work on and build for a lifetime? Do you love talking together in order to know and be known? Are you looking forward to fostering patterns of deep communication for life? Both of you have to be willing and able to make all other human relationships second to the marriage relationship. Does he respect you not only as a person, but also as a friend?

Also remember that when you become a wife, you become associated with a certain man. Your relationship with him means that your reputation is closely tied to his; even your last name will be the same. Does that excite you? Discourage you? Scare you? If he is a man at all worth marrying, that association will be something you can be proud of and thankful for. All husbands will goof up at some point, perhaps publicly. My very intelligent husband once locked the house so securely that the real estate agent was stuck outside for half an hour with potential buyers. That was uncomfortable, and every wife has a story like that. But on the whole, can you look forward to becoming Mrs. _____?

Some girls are attracted to marriage because they are afraid of the loneliness that singleness can bring. Pastor Jason Helopoulos warns us: 'Loneliness in a godless marriage can be even more severe than the loneliness one experiences in singleness.' Loneliness is no reason for marriage. And not every marriage solves loneliness. Do not allow your lack of close relationships with family and friends lock you into a hollow relationship with someone who will not be your best friend, confidant and lover.

Don't sacrifice the good relationships you have for the sake of one guy who can't value the people who love you. But don't marry someone who comes second to any other human relationship that you have. Marry someone whose relationship with you is strong and can nurture other relationships in your life. Marry someone who you can be happy to introduce to others as your husband because the relationship with him becomes the most valuable one you have.

7

What about Love?

You may have noticed that we have not yet talked about falling in love. We haven't asked whether you love the man you're with or not. That is because if he is not demonstrating the positive qualities that we have talked about, you have no business being in love with him.

This is radically counter-cultural for Westerners. We live in a culture that talks about falling in love as though it is ultimate, out of our control, and dictates what is right for us. But your emotional happiness is not of primary concern: your thankful obedience that brings glory to God is. The will of God is your sanctification (1 Thess. 4:3), not a romantic high. Also, although it might not seem like it in the moment, your long-term emotional happiness is only possible if these other aspects of your relationship are in order.

Because love (or what we think of when we think of love) is an emotion, it can come and go. Even a man who is madly in love with you will not be so constantly, at least not at that fever pitch. John Angell James warns: 'Charity [love] covers a multitude of faults, it is true; but we must not presume too far upon the credulity and blindness of affection; there is a point beyond which even love cannot be blind to the crimson coloring of a guilty action.'

If your emotional attraction and warm feeling for the person—your being 'in love'—evaporated at this moment, would Christian obedience and service and selflessness—your true love—pick up the dropped thread? In other words, if you wake up in five years and find a wet towel on the bathroom floor *again*, are you going to hang it up and talk about it calmly later, or will you be bitter or blow up? That's just a little thing; there will be bigger issues with bigger consequences that you have to deal with. When your husband is frustrating or infuriating, will you still see him as someone made in God's image and in humility consider him better than yourself (Phil. 2:3)? When you are bound in a covenantal, life-long relationship with your husband (marriage!), you have to!

In India, families often arrange marriages, and the divorce rate is more than 45 per cent lower than in America. People there generally come to marriage expecting it to be a relationship of duty, faithfulness, and work, with emotional attachments developing over time—quite the opposite of the Western stereotype. Lack of divorce does not mean happy marriages, though.

But then, neither does a rational decision to marry preclude love. Martin Luther, famous for being madly in love with his 'lord Katie', wrote years after his wedding that he did not love his wife at the start of their marriage: 'That came later.' Ann Judson, in her diary and letters, indicates that she agreed to marry her husband not because she was madly in love, but so that she could bring the gospel to women overseas. After the wedding, she grew deeply attached to her husband, who had loved her from the beginning. The very first marriage on earth was an arranged one (Gen. 2:22); we should not sneer at arranged or 'loveless' weddings with superior thoughts of romance.

God's definition

When our culture speaks about love, it usually means emotional attachment or physical attraction. We could do better than that and define it as 'an ever fixed mark/ That looks on tempests and is not shaken,' as Shakespeare did. Or we could do what we always should: go back to Scripture and see how the Bible defines it.

79

Back in the New Testament era, the Greek language had three words that people used for love: *eros*, *phileo* and *agapao*. The Bible never uses the first one (*eros*), which refers to sexual love and is the root of our word 'erotic.' It is a kind of love that wants something physical—the kind that is standard in Hollywood. It can come and go. In our world, it usually goes after a while.

Then there is *phileo*, which could be translated, 'being fond of.' It is the love of friendship. It is the kind of love that you have for a sister or a wonderful teacher. Non-Christian marriages are held together by this sort of love. It tends to hold on longer than *eros*, but it is often subject to our feelings and others' actions. When we have a biblical *phileo* it is a strong bond, as Scripture's standards for true friendship are high. It cannot weather every storm on its own, though.

But the third kind of love—*agapao*—is the kind of love that you need to sustain a Christian marriage through a lifetime. Lloyd-Jones writes:

> This (*agapao*) is the word that is always used in the Bible to express God's love to us. 'God so loved the world'— 'Agapao'… not an erotic feeling, not merely being fond of, it is the love that resembles God's love…The Apostle is addressing people who are filled with the Spirit, for they alone can show this love.

That is another reason that you must not marry a man who is not a Christian: he has not known this kind of love, he has refused this kind of love, and so he certainly cannot show you this kind of love.

Eros and *phileo* are to be present in a marriage. Delighting in God's gift of sexuality is part of a married couple's calling, and they should be attracted to one another in that way. Being fond of one another is also a kind of love that should be present. A Christian should not marry just any other Christian, but someone who is a friend, someone who is fond of them and not merely attracted to their body. Every decent non-Christian marriage has these two elements of love in them, but none has *agapao*.

Christ is the husband of every believer (Rom. 7:4). He loved us while we were yet sinners. God loved us when we were His enemies (Col. 1:21). His will for our lives is our sanctification: the beautification of our souls (1 Thess. 4:3). Christ gave Himself for us in love. God so loved the world that He gave His only begotten Son (John 3:16). The love of God—*agapao*—is a selfless, divine love. It is Spirit-empowered self-sacrifice, not based on what we do, nor what others do, but what Christ did for us.

And so, a Christian marriage must be based on and exhibit this kind of love. A believing husband, a believing wife, will in some measure demonstrate godly love: *agapao*. They will be willing to sacrifice self in order to show God's love to their spouse. A Christian lover will be enabled by the Spirit to lay down their life for the person whom God has given them in marriage. If you and a man are exhibiting *agapao* in addition to *eros* and *phileo*, then you have true love: that is marriage-worthy love.

Truly loving

'Love!' Derek Thomas says of the bride in the Song of Solomon:

> It has changed her perception of herself and given her worth, value. This is what love has done for her. She has begun to see herself as one who is loved and cherished, and that makes all the difference in the world.

> Those of us who are married know this experience well. We are amazed every day that someone should say they want to spend the rest of their lives with us—and they know us! And they are still saying, 'I want to spend the rest of my life with you; I want to grow old with you; I want to share my stories with you; I want to wake up in the morning and talk to you.'

That kind of love is only possible when grounded in grace, because only Christ-like grace can allow one person to know another person's failings, sins, faults, and still love them (Eph. 2:4-5).

The Puritans used to say, 'First you must choose your love. Then, you must love your choice.' It is the essentials that really count, because those are the things that you will be able to wisely choose and continue to love. We have not talked at all about a man's looks, taste in clothing, skills with Apple products, or ability to fix things around the house. That's because every man is going to get old and saggy. Every man's wife can encourage better fashion sense in her husband (if she's the one with the fashion sense!). And anyone can Google how to troubleshoot a tablet or install a toilet when they find themselves in a pinch.

If a certain skill or detail is very important to you, that is up to you. Some women (like me!) would find life difficult if their husband did not take care of the vehicle. That is a detail that the Lord blessed me with. But if you are willing to overlook essentials because you are in love with a detail (what he looks like, how cute his clothes are, etc.), that is foolish and it will end in grief.

Now, what you think about how he looks is not unimportant; you need to be attracted to whomever it is you're considering (or whoever is considering you)! But postmodern ideas about physical attraction, especially with the hookup culture that infests so many college and university campuses, are shallow and subjective and unrealistic. For our society, physical looks sometimes seem to be everything, when in reality they are only fleeting or lie in the eye of the beholder. So often, the saints we love in a non-romantic way become beautiful as we see their Christ-like character and experience their sacrificial love.

One couple we knew stood out for this: the husband was significantly better looking than the wife. She was average; he was unusually handsome. His love for her person and character blinded him to the difference; they were happily married with several sweet children. The opposite can happen, too. A beautiful woman can see through average looks to the amazing Christian man and they can be happily married. An average-looking man with stellar character is a far better choice than a good-looking man with average character. What matters in physical attraction is not where this man falls on the spectrum of 'most attractive' to 'least attractive', but whether or not you are attracted to this particular man and find him desirable.

Elizabeth Singer rejected the famous hymn-writer Isaac Watts' proposal of marriage, saying that she could not admire the casket as much as the jewel that it contained. In other words, she could not get past his poor looks and focus on his incredible Christian character. While it was right of her to not marry someone to whom she was not attracted, it does perhaps show spiritual immaturity on her part, that she could not see his Christian character shining so much that it brightened his looks. She passed by the opportunity to become one with an unusually godly and gifted man. Would you do the same?

As a Christian, you are called to love everyone; your neighbor, other believers, your enemies. So regardless of everything else, you are to show the love of Christ to everyone you meet and know. But as a Christian, you are to only be *in love* with someone who will be able to husband you in a biblical way— someone who will choose to love you even when you are in the wrong.

'As new creatures in Christ,' writes Baptist pastor Al Martin, 'we need to have our emotions informed by the light of the Word of God...Our emotions need objective truth to guide them, and the subjective power of the Holy Spirit must harness and channel them in a godly way.' Is Scripture directing and defining the love you have for someone? How about your boyfriend's professed love for you? Is it informed and directed by the Bible's parameters for a Christian relationship headed for marriage?

Nearly one thousand years ago, Peter Lombard wrote, '...woman was made from man, not from [just] any part of the man's body, but she was formed from his side, so that there might be shown, that she was created in a partnership of love, lest perchance, if she had been made from his head, she might seem to be preferred to man for his domination, or if from his feet, to be subject to him for his service. Therefore because for man there was prepared neither a lady [over a servant] nor a handmaid, but a companion, she was to be produced…from his side…that she might recognize that she was to be placed alongside him.' Centuries later, Matthew Henry would use those thoughts to observe: '[T]he woman was made of a rib out of the side of Adam; not made out of his head to rule over him, nor out of his feet to be trampled upon by him, but out of his side to be equal with him, under his arm to be protected, and near his heart to be beloved.' Does the man you are thinking of understand and demonstrate this love?

If you are in love with a person who is not godly and not growing in the fruit of the spirit, then you must end your emotional attachment to him, regardless of his interest in you. Might that be painful for everyone involved? Definitely. Is it right and necessary? Absolutely. Falling in love with someone is a choice you make; we have already talked about the consequences. Be very careful: do not be duped by the flashy details or put off by a plain exterior. Ask the Lord to give you the God-like ability to see the man's heart before you give him yours.

8

What about You?

Horatio Hornblower is the main character in C. S. Forester's novels of adventure in the British navy during the early nineteenth century. Horatio is a hero in every sense: clever, courageous, loyal, generous, honest, hardworking, kind, and (of course!) good-looking. After a few chapters (or an episode of the BBC series), you are convinced that he is the best officer the British Navy ever had, nevermind that he's fictitious. All he needs is a wife.

But Maria, the woman he ends up marrying out of a sense of pity and duty, is disappointing. She is not evil. She is not trying to climb the social ladder. She is not stupid. She is not anything in particular, and certainly not of the same calibre as her husband.

Merely because of her mediocrity, the wife is a drag on Hornblower. Readers of the novel are supposed to groan: 'If only he had waited for someone who could really have *helped* him—a woman whose love and companionship would have energized and been a delight to him!' He needed a helpmeet of the same calibre that he was. He didn't get one.

We've been thinking a lot about how a husband affects his wife. But how would you affect a husband? Because he is only one side of things; you are the other. Someone once told me that a mediocre man with a wonderful wife can become a great man, but a wonderful man with a bad wife can become less than a man. How would intimacy with you, spiritually, mentally, emotionally, physically, and relationally, affect a good man? Are *you* ready to be a godly wife? Let's think about that together.

Spiritually

Your spiritual condition will affect your husband just as much as his will affect you. Are you growing spiritually or have you leveled off, or are you struggling for some reason? Do you love God and commune with Him on your own, eagerly learning from His Word? If friends and shopping excite you more, you need to take stock of your priorities and prayerfully consider how to cultivate your spiritual tastes. These behavior patterns are not going to stop magically after marriage, and they spell spiritual difficulty for you and your husband if they continue.

Will you support and encourage your husband's initiative in leading family worship, or will you hinder it? Are you the type who is going to be up and getting the kids ready for worship on Sunday morning, or will your husband be struggling to get everyone in the car on time? Few men are capable of getting small children fed, dressed, and buckled into car seats by mid-morning without help, though God can grant grace in exceptional circumstances. And just because your husband is the leader in the relationship doesn't mean that he will be able to pull you along in sanctification. You will either be a drag on his holiness, or a catalyst, a sweet encouragement for his personal, spiritual development. That will also be true for any future children.

Can you take and give correction humbly and graciously? Katie Luther could listen to her husband's protests about her sharp tongue and still love him and work to change. That is not to excuse Luther's roughness, but to show that, in addition to the husband's godliness and devotion to his wife's soul, the wife must have a willingness to listen, despite less-than-perfect communication. Are you able to deal with the way in which your future husband will challenge your failings, or will you sulk if he does not handle you with kid gloves?

Are you excited at the thought of your husband's involvement in the local church? Are you going to encourage your husband to serve the congregation with his gifts, or will you complain that he's not helping with laundry instead? Are you going to free him up to build up the body of Christ in whatever ways he can, or are you going to make it the last priority? Are you a Priscilla (Acts 18) or a Michal (2 Sam. 6:16-20)? Are you right there beside your husband, encouraging his work for the Kingdom, or are you waiting at home to complain or mock? If you know that this will be an issue for you, then you have no business marrying a godly, servant-hearted man. Spiritual intimacy in marriage does not mean that he is at your beck and call because you, as his wife, have a biblical first claim to his time, energy, talents, and money. It means that as you both grow in grace together, gospel love will overflow from your home into the local church and community in a multitude of ways.

This is especially important to consider if the man you are considering is thinking about involvement in any sort of formal ministry. Far too many pastors are hindered in their work because of wives who take advantage of flexible work hours and a willingness to help—a characteristic of many ministry-minded men. These wives cripple the church. Their husbands are doing routine laundry instead of hospital visitation, ordinary child care instead of sermon preparation, and pampering their wives instead of shepherding souls.

My husband reviews a lot of recommendations for students applying to seminaries. Increasingly, good institutions and churches realize that not only the student, but also his wife, needs to be evaluated for ministry preparedness. An ordinary, faithful man shines with a steady, loving, wise and supportive wife. While you cannot qualify a husband for pastoral ministry, you can most certainly disqualify him. If you do, you will answer to God for keeping back one of His servants from laboring in the fields ripe for harvest. A wife has no right to ask her husband for his time or effort that belongs to God in Kingdom service. Free your husband up to gospel service as Susannah Spurgeon did her husband, seeing her sacrifice as a small thing when compared with the fruit it bore and the sacrifice which Christ had made for her.

We see that in 1 Kings 21:25, it tells us that Ahab's wife, Jezebel, was the one who incited him to much wickedness. The implication is that, without his wife, he would not have been such a curse to Israel and been responsible for the amount of evil he committed. Will intimacy with you bring your man spiritual good and blessing instead of drawing him away from Christ? What steps are you taking to cultivate your own spiritual life so as to be best prepared to lovingly support your husband?

Emotionally

While the average woman tends to be more emotional than the average man, that does not mean that men have no emotional needs. So, how will you encourage your husband in his work, as you expect him to encourage you in yours? What will you be able to do for him to boost his spirits when he is down? Are you ready to join in his joys with enthusiasm, or will he be alone in them? Are you ready to sympathize with his frustrations, or will you be giving him an 'Uh-huh' over your shoulder while you tweak your Pinterest?

What about your tongue? What do you say about your potential husband to your girlfriends? Your mother? Facebook and Twitter-world? I knew a woman who repeatedly belittled her husband, not as an evil man, not as a bad father, but as an inept goof. It was this woman's habit to talk this way, and it made people disrespect her husband. While it is a husband's responsibility to behave in a respectable way, it is a wife's responsibility to speak of him in a way that preserves and builds up his reputation, instead of revealing his shortcomings and faults to the world. The Proverbs 31 woman behaved and spoke in a way that enabled her husband to trust her fully (v. 11). She did him good, not harm, all the days of her life (v. 12), partly with her words.

That does not mean that a wife should be hiding her husband's serious patterns of sin from pastors or other people who need to know. It does mean that she must be very careful to speak respectfully wherever possible about her husband. Will you build up your man's reputation or tear it down? Will you teach any future children to respect him, or will you teach them by your example to think little of him? Will you broadcast every failure that your husband has, or will you, in love, hide them from the world and help him fight them in private, with pastoral help if necessary? What will you do for your husband's reputation?

Will you strive to cultivate contentment? A discontented wife is a huge burden for a husband. Can you be happy with the social status, income, clothes, and conversation that come with the man of whom you are thinking? If not, it is either a case of unusually serious heart issues with contentment (which is a struggle for almost all of us), or a case of a very poor match.

Physically

Though we know what Scripture says about being the weaker vessel in a one-flesh relationship, we do contribute considerably to the physical aspect of a relationship. Respecting and submitting to a husband does not mean you do not care for him. Are you going to encourage him to exercise and prepare decent food for him to help him maintain his physical health? We should not be worrying about six-packs, but we should be helping our husbands care for their bodies as temples of the Holy Spirit.

God created Eve to be a help suitable for Adam—a helpmeet (Gen 2:18ff.). She is a pattern for all other wives. Are you excited about the work that your boyfriend does or hopes to do, or do you not care? Are you able to help him where possible, or would you rather not be involved? The sort of help that a wife/helpmeet provides partly depends on her husband's calling, but it should always be there. There are examples of this everywhere: a husband who lays flooring and goes through the knees of his pants has a wife who loves beautiful floors and keeps him supplied with new work jeans. A husband who is an accountant and works long hours every tax season has a wife who keeps dinner hot for him and has the kids in bed when he gets home. A minister who faces spiritual opposition has a wife who listens and encourages. A small town doctor has a wife who figures out how to get bodily fluids out of scrubs.

But I also know men whose wives hate their work; these women frustrate their husbands in their callings. It's a huge burden to the men, stunting them in their careers and the use of their gifts.

Can you help your future husband? Do you want to? Marriage is not going to make your life easier and simpler. Quite the opposite. It might be better, but it won't be effortless. Are you ready for that?

What would happen if your husband's work required you to move away from your family, friends, and church? Are you going to pout and protest and put on a martyr complex? Or will you understand that this is part of leaving and cleaving (Gen. 2:24): being one and going through life together? Will you facilitate a move, even if it is hard? Can you be a helpmeet through that situation?

A large part of helping your husband is taking care of the home, children, and bearing the burden of domestic care. There are situations where this is not possible, but for most Christian wives, it should be the norm. This sounds terribly old-fashioned, though it is slowly coming back into vogue with the rise of the 'yummy mummy'. But are you willing and able to do it for biblical reasons: because you believe that it is the general pattern of Scripture and blesses your family (Titus 2:5; 1 Tim. 5:9-10)? Do you have the self-control and discipline to limit Facebook, Pinterest, phone time, and any other distractions so that you can be a help to your husband in this way?

What will you do with the money that your husband earns through his work? Will you go shopping all the time, or wisely budget? Will you ask your husband for advice about financial decisions or make big changes without considering him? Are you reckless with money or can you enable your family to live within your means, perhaps even below them? If you are marked by greediness instead of an eagerness to give sacrificially to the work of the church, that is a serious problem. Greedy wives have torn marriages apart. Do you look now for ways to get extra money, or are you finding ways to bless others in need with what you have? Present use of money is an indicator of future contentment and wisdom in a marriage.

The marriage service vows make it clear that you are to be faithful to your husband 'in sickness and in health'. Are you ready and willing to care for him when he is down with the flu or some other small illness? It's easy to think, 'Get a grip. It's a cold; I'm facing childbirth.' But that does not help either of you. Are you willing to care for him? These little trials and tests may be preparation for lengthy and even terminal illnesses. Providence calls many wives to care for their husbands as their bodies break down in old age. Are you willing to sacrifice your comfort and convenience and much more to be faithful in that situation? Is he the sort of boyfriend that you can respect to that extent after the honeymoon? Don't wait until then to decide.

What about physical protection? Many men think that chivalry is old-fashioned. Do you? Will you welcome this expression of his love for you, this opportunity he has to cherish you? Or will you shrug it off, maybe even become irritated when he communicates his care for you in this way?

Intimacy also means sexual oneness. Are you going to be sexually available, within reason, or will you use your body as a tool of manipulation to get your husband to do what you want? Are you going to begrudgingly approach the marriage bed, or will you treat it as a good gift that God has given the two of you to enjoy, as an expression of love and delight and God's means for bringing children into the world? A wife who sees sex as a bargaining tool or a dirty job to get over with is not thinking biblically.

Sexual and romantic faithfulness is also something that we need to take seriously as we consider becoming wives. Often, the burden of this is placed on the men. That is as it should be, since they are the leaders, initiators, and tend to struggle more with lust. But that does not get us off the hook, because there are ways that we are prone to infidelity. Are you ready to be faithful to one man until one of you is dead? That does not only mean that you cannot sleep with other men. It also means that we are mentally and emotionally faithful to our husbands. Perhaps that is as difficult for us as physical lust is for them, as romance is so attractive to us and can seem so innocent. Are you willing to turn your eyes and your heart away from the man who is flirting with you? How about the romantic movie or novel? Are you willing to sacrifice any or all of those if they tempt you to think about what it would be like to be in a relationship with the guy on the screen or the page? Wishing you could marry Mr. Knightley is in the same category, though not the same degree, as sleeping with the neighbor. Are you prayerfully going to love *your* husband actively and just as actively kill the smallest thoughts that tempt you to not love him exclusively?

Think about your body for a minute. Are you willing to maintain your physical health and decent appearance by exercising and eating moderate amounts of nutritious food? That is part of caring for your body, which is a temple of the Holy Spirit (1 Cor. 6:19): wise stewardship of the resources of body and health. It is also kindness to a husband to try and maintain physical health and levels of energy so that you can be a helpmeet. It is a sign of your love for him to try and keep your body attractive to him. This is done within reason, of course, knowing that age and childbearing take their toll. Beauty is fleeting (Prov. 31:30). But that does not mean that we can 'let ourselves go', making our husbands deal with our extra weight or our inability to keep up with the kids because we're out of breath. It is as self-absorbed to obsess about your physical appearance as it is to ignore it because of laziness or love of food. Caring for your body by eating wisely and staying in shape will enable you to be a helpmeet to your husband as you encourage and facilitate his care for the body God gave him, too. Are you willing to do that?

Mentally

T. S. Eliot's 1922 poem 'The Wasteland' describes a wife who tries to extract her husband's thoughts and feelings by force: 'Speak to me. Why do you never speak? Speak./What are you thinking of? What thinking? What?' Are you prepared to give your husband mental peace even when you would like to get inside his head? Scripture gives us so many warnings about nagging, pestering, quick-tempered wives (Gen. 30:1-2; Prov. 21:9, 19; 25:24). Men married to women like these are willing to live on a roof in order to have some mental peace! Will you prayerfully work to not be that woman? John Angell James states that 'There must be no searching after faults, nor examining with microscopic scrutiny… no reproachful epithets; no rude contempt; no incivility; no cold neglect.' Are you already careful to not pester and nag, and mentally wear your man down, or will you prevent frustration where you can by graciously expressing your opinion and being content with his leadership?

Are you going to respect your husband and tell him so, or will you treat him like one of the kids? In our culture, movies, books and TV depict husbands as incompetent goofs (when they are not abusers and adulterers) who need wives to run their lives and make sure they don't get the family into a mess. Have you bought into that stereotype? A lack of respect from a wife can take a huge toll on a man's mental condition. But true, appropriately expressed respect for your husband can strengthen and encourage him to pursue his role with even more zeal.

Relationally

Think about your future husband's relationships—the ones that bless him and bring him joy. Are you willing to help and enable him to maintain and develop these? Do you respect his parents? Are you happy to have them as grandparents for your children? If they are domineering and interfering people, are you on the same page as their son as to how you can graciously deal with that? Your husband's family will have an effect on your marriage, for better or for worse, and so will your responses to those relationships. Marriage will bring you into relationship with them. Does the man you're thinking of marrying have parents who will make your relationship impossible? Are you willing to suddenly have a close relationship with people who are near-strangers now? Are you willing to work on a relationship with them for the sake of your marriage and simple Christian love?

What about his male friends and mentors? Will you encourage the man you have in mind to be accountable to older godly men, or do you not care, and complain that they are intruding into your lives? Will you suggest that he calls up your brother once in a while and see how he's doing, or will you whine that he's not spending that free time with you? Will you be happy on occasion to put the kids to bed alone so he can visit with a friend, or will you not give him that opportunity? If not, you have no business saying, 'I do.'

So how will *you* do after the vows? You have just as much potential to build or ruin a marriage as a man does. What we've talked about here is just a sampling of the ways that a wife can bless or curse her husband. The effects are far-reaching, long-lasting, and either wonderful or difficult. Of course, there is no perfect woman. You will not reach perfect holiness until glory. But you can make huge advances in sanctification in this earth. God loves to answer His people's pleas for holiness.

I know men whose careers, families, personal development and even congregations have been destroyed by their wives. It's heartbreaking and messy, especially for the husband, but judgment will come to the wife for her own unrepented sin. If you're not ready to be married, don't get married and put your spouse in a painful situation that is 100 per cent avoidable. Don't marry someone whose leadership you can't follow. Don't marry someone who will be stunted in their spiritual growth, personhood, and fruitfulness because of you. Don't get married if you cannot do the work of a wife in a way that merits at least some encouragement or public praise (Prov. 31:31).

We also need to remember that we are partly responsible for the way in which a husband treats us. We can facilitate or discourage his godly behavior by ours. Scripture has given us so much counsel on living humbly and lovingly with others, especially husbands, that we cannot complain about a lack of instruction. John Angell James reminds us, 'If therefore, we would be respected, we should be respectable.' The same is true for love: if we want to be loved, we must be loving and lovable. If we want to have a husband who is our friend, we must be friendly. If our husband is called to lead and shepherd us, we must be willing to follow. True, our husbands cannot blame their poor leadership and behavior on us. Their sin is their fault. But if we make it difficult or discouraging for them to be the husbands that God calls them to be, God will call us to account. Now that's a sobering thought!

Through this book, we have tried to think deeply about whether the man measures up. If he does not— if he is not a believer, or if he is but his trajectory is in an unhealthy direction—we need to look elsewhere for a spouse. But if *we* do not measure up, we have no business accepting the attentions of a superior man. What does your trajectory look like? Is it similar to the trajectory of the man whom you are considering? Will your trajectory drag down his? Or will it give it a boost?

If you prayerfully look at your life and see that your spiritual immaturity or emotional needs or expectations for money and time or intellectual ability or any other aspect of your life will stunt or hinder a mature man who has shown interest in you, then the wise thing to do is sever ties with him. Unless you can honestly say that you are a help*meet* (a helper fit for that particular man), you have no right to say 'I do.'

It may be that you are already aware of certain spiritual, emotional, physical, or relational issues that hinder you and that are tied to your family of origin or other formative experiences. Though it is important to acknowledge these influences and pray for deliverance from them, I encourage you not to use your background as an excuse for your own sins. You may need help with struggles, but you cannot pin your own sins on others' actions. Many people look up to Katie Luther as the model wife of the Reformation. Fewer people know that her mother died when she was young; her father and step-mother essentially donated her to a convent which sent her off to another convent years later. Once converted, she asked her family to rescue her and was refused. After her escape she lived as a servant with a Protestant family and was the last of the freed nuns to fall in love; the fellow abandoned her under pressure from his parents. She finally married Martin Luther, who asked her to be his wife so he could 'spite the Pope and the Devil, please his father, and set an example of matrimony'. If anyone could blame their past, it was Katie. And yet we find her butchering pigs, hosting students, teaching children, reading manuscripts and tending to 'Herr Doctor'. We are accountable for the way in which we respond to our past, even when we were sinned against. Part of being a godly woman is understanding the difficulties in our past and trusting that God will deliver us from bondage to sinful patterns. This takes honesty and, as Katie models, diligence.

Fairy-tale marriages do not happen when the wife has a princess complex and is always waiting for her knight in shining armor to come and rescue her. But biblical marriages happen when the wife is willing to work hard to be a helpmeet fit for the man whom she has married so that both husband

and wife can serve, put sin to death, and bring glory to God. Do you realize that marriage will make your life more complicated because you will be doing your own work and helping a husband with his? Are you prepared for sacrificial giving, compromising, being tired without complaining, forgiving and asking for forgiveness, and doing lots of hard work without praise? If not, please don't get married yet.

There have been a few fathers in history who refused to give their daughters in marriage to wonderful men because the fathers realized that their daughters would slow the suitors' fruitfulness. These fathers realized that the suitors were men whose level of personal gifts and piety would be hampered by their own daughters' gifts and piety. They realized that their daughters would ruin the suitors' callings, so they ended the relationships. Many of these fathers were Christian, and had the good of Christ's Bride, the church, at heart. That allowed them to protect suitors from unsuitable wives, even if that meant giving up a stellar son-in-law. Martin Luther raised his orphaned niece and loved her like a father, but told a godly suitor, 'I know, of course, that [Lena] would be taken care of with you. I don't know, however, whether you would be taken care of with her.' He advised the young man to marry someone better, which he did.

That is putting Christ first. That is seeking first His Kingdom. That is the sort of honesty and selflessness that we need to develop and look for in our parents and mentors.

If you answer these questions and feel inadequate, that's a good sign! We are all inadequate, as we fail to measure up to the standard of holiness that Christ demonstrated and calls us to. We all need the Holy Spirit to enable us to be godly wives. But, just like a man who wants to become a spouse, you should not need counsel for basic personality issues, and a healthy trajectory is vital. If you are bothered by the questions above because you think that you have these basic issues, or that your life's trajectory is unhealthy, then your conscience is honestly telling you where you are at. The awareness of your own failings means that you can prayerfully use the means of grace to grow in grace. If you have the humility to confess that you are not ready to get married, not ready to become one with a godly man, then you are in a good position: God gives grace to the humble; He loves to save them (Ps. 18:27), lead them (25:9), and give them His favor and wisdom (Prov. 3:34; 11:2). If you feel inadequate, take heart. A willingness to ask for advice and die to self are the biggest assets in being a godly wife. All of us need humility and help as we grow in conformity to God's high calling to us (Prov. 31).

We are sinners and we marry sinners. It's grace that keeps any couple faithful till death.

Pursue holiness and godliness as ends apart from any relationship goals and you will be getting the best preparation for marriage that a person can possibly have: preparation that will fit you to be a help-meet for someone who is Christ-like. That is the kind of man to whom you can submit and help, not perfectly, but increasingly well, by grace.

Luther once observed:

> Next to God's Word, the world has no more precious treasure than holy matrimony. God's best gift is a pious, cheerful, God-fearing wife, with whom you may live peacefully, to whom you may entrust your goods, your body, and your life.

Will you prayerfully work to be and become that sort of a wife?

Conclusion

John Angell James states: 'The privacies of [marriage] lay open our motives, and all the interior of our character; so that we are better known to each other than we are to ourselves.' There is no hiding in marriage: not for you, not for your husband. The good, the bad, and the ugly are all laid right out and will shape the rest of your life. The seeds of each of these issues is almost always there before the marriage. While you are dating, you can get glimpses of his care for your intellectual growth and spiritual health, or his physical abuse and emotional neglect.

So how will your boyfriend do after the vows? Because this is just a sampling of the ways that a husband can bless or curse his wife. The effects are far-reaching, long-lasting, and either wonderful or difficult. True, there are no perfect men out there. But there are great ones. Beware of the ones that are not.

Marriage to the wrong person is a nightmare. I've been in a church parking lot where the pastor had to call the police to protect a wife from her husband. Years before, she had been warned against marrying him, but went ahead. Then she needed physical protection from a husband who was trying to stop her from worshipping with her family. This was an ugly and frightening scene, and though this is a dramatic and public example, perhaps the scenes that we never know about are equally difficult and devastating to those involved. I urge you: don't be so desperate to get married that your marriage is a grief. Don't marry someone whose leadership you can't follow. Don't marry someone who is not seeking to love you as Christ loved the church.

Do not look for a spouse who will merely be an equal independent adult, or a business partner with a prenuptial in case of divorce, or someone who likes to go on the same rides that you do at the amusement park. None of these are criteria for choosing a spouse. At best, you will have a fully functioning roommate who shares many of your tastes and interests but never becomes one with you in the mysterious way that Paul describes in

Ephesians 5. Those sorts of relationships lack the 'tenderness of love, supported by esteem and guided by politeness' that John Angell James holds up as the ideal.

Derek Thomas says, 'If you seek short-term profits in a relationship, you are in real danger... When you enter into a marriage relationship, be prepared for the consequences. Though the short-term view of a relationship may entice you, you must take account of the long-term view, because you will spend the rest of your life with this person.' If you ignore the counsel of Scripture and those around you, you will have no one to blame for a bad relationship but yourself.

The Bible describes this life as a journey (Ps. 84:5-7), as a war (Eph. 6:11-17), and as a race (Heb. 12:1). While physical attraction and the ability to provide are musts, good looks and special skills don't ultimately matter, do they? Marry someone who will help you on your spiritual pilgrimage as it becomes your shared spiritual pilgrimage. Marry someone who will be a fellow soldier in the war against sin and self and Satan as you take back enemy territory together, dependent on the Lord as one. Marry someone who will run beside you towards immortality, eternal life and that crown of glory.

Spiritual intimacy with Christ brings ultimate blessing. Marrying someone who will love you as

Christ loved the church will bring you foretastes and pictures and little parts of that larger blessing. It will also draw you closer to it. If you are someone who knows and demonstrates the love of Christ, marry someone else who knows and demonstrates the love of Christ. That is the only way that two sinners bound together in intimacy for life can thrive.

And let's remember that if we do marry an amazing, godly man, it's not as result of our brilliant wisdom or keen perception; it's a blessing from the Lord. Regardless of whether we are a witness to Christ in a bad marriage, or if we are enjoying a redeemed marriage, or if we married someone incredible and are happily working on building the marriage, it's all by God's grace, and God gets all the glory. God is most glorified when we are growing in grace: loving Him with all our hearts, souls, minds, and strength, and our neighbor as ourselves. Good marriages best equip us do this, and that is what brings God the most glory. And that's really what it's all about, isn't it?

In a way, the question, 'How do I know who God wants me to marry?' is much simpler than we think. The will of God is our sanctification. So, the next time a godly man who makes you want to be more like Jesus asks you to marry him, it's probably a good idea to say 'Yes!'

Appendix

Bibliography

Adams, Jay. *Marriage, Divorce, and Remarriage in the Bible: A Fresh Look at What Scripture Teaches.* Grand Rapids: Zondervan, 1980.

Book of Common Prayer. Toronto: Anglican Book Centre, 1959.

Butterfield, Rosaria Champagne. *Secret Thoughts of an Unlikely Convert.* Pittsburgh: Crown and Covenant, 2012.

Eliot, Elizabeth. *Let Me Be a Woman.* Wheaton, IL: Tyndale, 1976.

Eliot, T. S. 'The Wasteland' in *The Norton Anthology of English Literature.* New York: W. W. Norton & Company, 1975.

Gouge, William. *Domestical Duties*. London: John Haviland for William Bladen, 1622.

Hamilton, Ian. Sermons on the Song of Solomon. Cambridge Presbyterian Church, June 13–September 5, 2010. http://www.cambridgepres.org.uk/sermons/song.html. Accessed June 25, 2013.

Haykin, Michael, ed. *The Christian Lover: The Sweetness of Love and Marriage in Letters of Believers.* Lake Mary, FL: Reformation Trust, 2009.

Helopoulos, Jason. 'Singles and Loneliness' on *Kevin DeYoung: DeYoung, Restless and Reformed.* http://thegospelcoalition.org/blogs/kevindeyoung/2013/07/02/singles-and-loneliness/. Accessed July 9, 2013.

Henry, Matthew. *Commentary on the Whole Bible*. Nashville: Thomas Nelson, 1997.

James, John Angell. *A Help to Domestic Happiness*. Morgan, PA: Soli Deo Gloria, 1995.

James, Sharon. *My Heart in His Hands: Ann Judson of Burma.* Darlington, U.K. Evangelical Press, 1998.

Kelleman, Robert. *Sexual Abuse: Beauty for Ashes*. Phillipsburg, NJ: P&R Publishing, 2013.

Kroker, Ernst. *The Mother of the Reformation: The Amazing Life and Story of Katharine Luther*, trans.

Mark E. DeGarmeaux. St. Louis: Concordia, 2013.

Li, Jeanette. *Jeanette Li: The Autobiography of a Chinese Christian*. Edinburgh: Banner of Truth, 1971.

Lloyd-Jones, Martyn. *Christian Marriage: From Basic Principles to Transformed Relationships.* Edinburgh: Banner of Truth, 2012. Formerly published as *Life in the Spirit in Marriage, Home and Work.* Grand Rapids: Baker Books, 1995.

Lombard, Peter. 'On the Creation and Formation of Things Corporal and Spiritual and Many Others Pertaining to This' in *The Four Books of Sentences*, trans. Alexis Bugnolo. http://www.franciscan-archive.org/lombardus/II-Sent.html. Accessed August 29, 2013.

Mahaney, Carolyn. *Feminine Appeal.* Wheaton, IL: Crossway, 2003.

Martin, Albert N. *Grieving, Hope and Solace: When a Loved One Dies in Christ.* Adelphi, MD: Cruciform Press, 2011.

Owen, John. *The Mortification of Sin.* Tain, Fearn, U. K.: Christian Focus Publications, 1996.

Philips, Richard D. *The Masculine Mandate: God's Calling to Men.* Lake Mary, FL: Reformation Trust, 2010.

Robertson, O. Palmer. *The Genesis of Sex*. Phillips-burg, NJ: P&R Publishing, 2002.

Shakespeare, William. 'Sonnet 116' in *The Norton Anthology of English Literature*. New York: W. W. Norton & Company, 1975.

Spencer, Edmund. 'Epithalamion' in *The Norton Anthology of English Literature*. New York: W. W. Norton & Company, 1975.

Thomas, Derek and Rosemary. *A Biblical Guide to Love, Sex and Marriage*. Faverdale North, U. K.: Evangelical Press, 2007.

Resources for a struggling marriage.

Perhaps you picked up this book sometime after you said your vows. I have had many, many e-mails from men and women who wished that they had thought through these things more carefully, but are now married. Thoughts like this are common: 'If only I could reverse time to eight years ago, and give this book to my newly engaged self. But I didn't, and now I am in a terrible marriage. What am I supposed to do *now*?' Perhaps your marriage was strong once, but is not any more. Perhaps it's been a struggle since your honeymoon. If you are a believer whose marriage is unhealthy either because your husband is a weak Christian or an unbeliever, or because you have not been the wife that God has called you to be (which is all of us), there are resources for you.

The means of grace—the Word, prayer, sacraments, and Christian fellowship—are essential for your marriage, just as they are for every believer. This means that if you profess faith in Christ, if you believe that His substitutionary atonement on the cross took the penalty for your sins, opening the way for you to be adopted into God's family, then you need to join God's people who are your brothers and sisters in a local congregation. Membership in a Bible-believing church that you can attend weekly is the first step.

In a local congregation where the Bible is faithfully taught, baptism and the Lord's Supper are biblically administered, and church discipline is lovingly carried out, you will receive the teaching, support and accountability that you need for spiritual health and strength. It will also be a protected place to bring any children that you have; a place where they will also be loved and taught and shepherded. The local church should also be your first stop for counseling. There, in a place where you are known and loved, you can hear biblical truth applied to your life.

Depending on the level of difficulty you are experiencing, there are good books that can help you along. Carolyn Mahaney's book, *Feminine Appeal*, has wise words that help us see where we can be better wives—more conformed to the pattern of inner beauty and selflessness that we see Christ exemplify. O. Palmer Robertson's *Genesis of Sex* goes through the first book of the Bible, looking at many of the instances of sexuality that Moses describes and drawing out principles for today's relationships. Robertson very pastorally discusses being in a loveless marriage, rape, divorce, and other difficult situations, all while keeping the gospel in view. *Sexual Abuse: Beauty for Ashes*, by Robert Kelleman, helps victims of sexual abuse think through the issues and implications that come with this tragedy. Using the biblical story of Amnon and Tamar, he walks victims through the struggles that come with such terrible experiences and helps them find healing at the cross.

But a solid church and biblical books will not fix the problem by themselves. If you are hiding a bad marriage from those around you, please stop. Hiding the struggles, little or big, will not solve them. If you have humbly confronted your spouse about damaging patterns of sin and there has been no willingness to repent and change, then you have a duty to bring it before other believers (Matt. 18).

I heard from one man the sad consequences of not doing that: he covered up his wife's high spending and child abuse for years until it was too late. His grown children are a mess; he has to pay off tens of thousands of dollars in credit card debt and is a shell of a man. The same is true for women who cover up bad marriages: they can suffer years of abuse, watch their children being abused, and live like caged animals. Start rescuing your marriage by telling someone you trust about the patterns of unrepented sin now, even if you think they are small. If they are not dealt with, they almost always grow.

If you or your children are suffering abuse at the hands of your husband, please go to the police right away. If that feels like too big a step for you to take, go to whomever you feel comfortable going to and let them help you from there. There is help for you; you can be protected and brought to a safe place where your abuser cannot hurt you or your children any more. If someone like a police officer or a pastor or a mother or sister is encouraging you to press charges for physical abuse, please take it seriously, and allow justice to take its course.

It is hard to press charges against someone you love, even when they are abusing you. But to not press charges is to allow them to continue in great sin without having to consider the consequences. Use legal means to stop this man in his wickedness, for his own good as well as yours. Allowing abuse to continue also puts yourself and your children at great risk—realize that safety and freedom are available and that you have a duty to pursue them. There is no shame for you in exposing this, only the opportunity to live without fear. This is especially true if you are a mother; do not fail to offer your children the protection that they have a right to.

Please realize that you are not the only Christian wife in a difficult marriage. In the cloud of witnesses that Hebrews describes, there are many faithful women whom God enabled to be faithful, and who have received the crown of glory. Jeanette Li was a twentieth-century Chinese Christian who had an unusually difficult life: married off very young to an adulterous husband, abused by her mother-in-law, kept from her children, then converted and ostracized, she nevertheless led a remarkably fruitful life in the middle of a bloody time in Chinese history. I know women in a variety of situations who are being faithful: a woman who divorced her adulterous husband and married a wonderful pastor; a woman who decided to remain married to her adulterous husband and has received grace for her marriage; a woman who is married to an unbeliever and finds spiritual strength and support in a local congregation; a woman who divorced her abusive husband to protect her children and has a wonderful relationship with her parents and siblings. Whatever your situation, God has provided the means of grace to free you from the power of sin and to walk in His light and His truth. I encourage you to look for the means of deliverance and support that He is providing you even if your marriage seems dark or dim.

The Heidelburg Catechism reminds us that our only comfort in life and in death is that we are not our own, but belong in body and soul, both in life and death, to our faithful Savior Jesus Christ. He has fully paid for our sins with His precious blood and delivered us from all the power of the devil; He also watches over us in such a way that not a hair can fall from our heads without the will of our Father in Heaven. In fact, all things must be subservient to our salvation. Therefore, by His Holy Spirit, He also assures us of eternal life, and makes us ready and willing from now on to live for Him. If your marriage is troubled, please get help. While you do, you can trust Christ's care for you and be assured that in Him, your eternity will be spent in glory.

Finding a local church

Because a faithful, local congregation is so important to your spiritual health, finding a good one is vital. But doing an internet search for local churches can be hazardous—picking a church can be as tricky as finding a husband!

There are places that call themselves churches that have no business doing so because they deny the Lordship of Christ, who is the Head of the church. This would include all sects and cults, such as the Jehovah's Witnesses or the Mormons. They deny the Trinity—the deity of Jesus—and so leave their followers with an unbiblical, finite, imperfect mediator who cannot cover all their sins before God. A church that accepts human teaching as having equal authority with Scripture, such as the Pope's, is also one that we should avoid.

There are three marks of a true church: preaching, sacraments and discipline. Preaching that explains the Word of God simply, clearly, and applies it to the hearts of those listening is what we need. A true church will have a man faithfully preaching and a congregation seeking to listen and obey. The two sacraments of baptism and the Lord's Supper are also correctly ministered in a true church: given by ordained men to the people of God in an orderly, regular way. Discipline, the loving, sad process by which church members are warned when they fall into sin, is the third mark of a true church.

If you need a place to get started in finding a church, there are some websites that are helpful. If you live in the U. S. or Canada, the denominational homepages of the Associate Reformed Presbyterian Church (also in Mexico and Pakistan), the Orthodox Presbyterian Church, the Lutheran Church (Missouri Synod), the Reformed Presbyterian Church (also in the U. K. and parts of east Asia) and the Presbyterian Church of America are helpful. If you are in North America and hold Baptist convictions, Sovereign Grace Ministries and 9Marks are useful places to start locating a faithful church near you. Outside of North America are many more denominations and church groups; some will differ in their faithfulness in different geographical areas. Anglican churches in the U. K. are not often faithful, but ones in many African countries often are. Reading websites and putting pastors' names into search engines can help you get a good idea of what a particular congregation is like.

Perhaps the best way to find a local church is to memorize the three marks, then start going to services with your Bible open. Be like the Bereans, who examined the Scriptures to make sure they were hearing the real gospel from God's Word (Acts 17:11). Ask the Lord to give you a church where you can worship, be fed, shepherded, and grow with God's people. He died for the church— He loves to build it up and bring people into it!

Study Questions

1. Spend some time thinking and praying about a Christian view of marriage. Write out this view in your own words and discuss it with a mentor. Why is it biblical? How is it different from the view of marriage that the world presents?

2. What is submission? Why does it matter in a marriage?

3. What role does culture play in a relationship? What sorts of everyday things are affected by someone's cultural background? What sorts of 'big' issues are there, such as language, gender roles, etc.?

4. The marriages that we grow up watching influence us more than we know, especially our parents' relationship. What sort of messages have those

marriages impressed upon you? Have they conveyed positive, biblical impressions about leadership and submission, sexual fidelity, raising children, etc.? Why or why not?

5. What are two ways that you can strengthen ties with your local congregation in order to be a part of the fellowship, take part in the means of grace, and have loving accountability?

6. Read one of the biographies listed in the bibliography. What aspect of that marriage would you most like to repeat in your own? Are there any aspects you would like to avoid?

7. What sort of attitude has your boyfriend demonstrated towards children? Does he notice them? Interact with them? Look up to godly fathers as role models? What makes you think so?

8. Think about your boyfriend's relationship with his mother. Would you be comfortable being treated the way he treats her in her home? Why or why not?

9. Ask your parents, pastor, or a mentor what they think will be the hardest aspect of being a helpmeet for you. Do you agree or did you come up with a different one?

10. If possible, attend the church where your boyfriend is a member. Do people know him there? What do they think of him? How is he involved? Why?

11. Do you love and trust this man enough to leave your father and mother and become one with him, perhaps moving far away from family and friends? Do you have good reason to believe that he would be supportive in a new or different environment, and would you be proud to support him as well?

12. Are you and your boyfriend studying God's Word and praying together? Why or why not? How?

13. Go on a 'service date': babysit a large family together; do yard work for a widow; clean the house for a new mother; or ask your deacons for some other idea. What is your boyfriend's work ethic like in practice? Did you work well as a team? Did he show selflessness towards others? What issues came up? How did you work through them?

14. What aspect of your boyfriend's personality bothers you the most? Are you ready to graciously live with that for a lifetime? Have you discussed this with him and are you taking any steps to work together in dealing with each other's concerns or aggravations?

15. Of all the chapters and principles in this book, which stand out to you as the most likely to be potential problems in the relationship you're currently in? If you're not in a dating relationship at the moment, which chapters or principles taught you something new about what you should think about or expect from a potential mate? How will you build on these insights as you grow in Christ and seek personal maturity?